THE REMINISCENCES OF
Captain Arthur R. Hawkins
U.S. Navy (Retired)

INTERVIEWED BY
Paul Stillwell

U.S. Naval Institute • Annapolis, Maryland

Copyright © 1996

Preface

This oral history with Captain Ray Hawkins was the fortuitous result of an interview trip to Pensacola several years ago. When I inquired at the Naval Aviation Museum, as it was then known, about likely candidates for interviews, Captain Hawkins's name was suggested immediately. He compiled an outstanding record as a fighter pilot during World War II and then went on to a varied and interesting career as a naval officer.

Captain Hawkins's oral history differs from many of those in the Naval Institute collection in that he was not a Naval Academy graduate. In 1942, he came in as an aviation cadet and then won his wings through an accelerated training program, because the Navy needed pilots to man the many new aircraft carriers being turned out by American shipyards. Once in action in the Pacific in 1944, Captain Hawkins recorded 14 kills against Japanese aircraft while flying the F6F Hellcat. During the Korean War, flying the F9F-2 Panther, he was involved in the earliest use of Navy jets as bombers. He had two tours of duty with the Blue Angels, the Navy's prestigious flight demonstration team. In 1953, while the skipper of the Blue Angels, he made the first through-the-canopy ejection and survived. Interspersed with tours of shore duty, Captain Hawkins commanded an attack squadron, a carrier air group, and a fleet oiler. He became a specialist in programming during the Robert McNamara years in the Pentagon, and he had a satisfying tour as commanding officer of the U.S. Naval Air Station, Atsugi, Japan.

In the course of moving from the initial raw transcript of the oral interviews to this final version, both Captain Hawkins and I have done some editing in the interests of accuracy, smoothness, and clarity. I have added footnotes to provide further information for readers using the volume. Captain Hawkins has given his blessing to this completed version. Ms. Ann Hassinger of the Naval Institute's history division has made a significant contribution through her diligence in the overall process of printing, proofreading, and overseeing the binding of the completed volume.

Paul Stillwell
Director, History Division
U.S. Naval Institute
September 1996

CAPTAIN ARTHUR RAY HAWKINS
UNITED STATES NAVY (RETIRED)

Arthur Ray Hawkins was born in Zavalla, Texas, on 12 December 1922, son of Alva M. and Gillie B. (Russell) Hawkins. He attended Lon Morris College in Jacksonville, Texas, and in 1939-40 was an aerial photographer for the American Automobile Association, mapping the states. On 29 April 1942, he enlisted in the U.S. Naval Reserve as a seaman second class. He had cadet training at the naval air stations in Dallas and Corpus Christi, Texas. He was designated a naval aviator and commissioned ensign, to date from 1 January 1943. He was subsequently promoted with the following dates of rank: lieutenant (junior grade), 1 March 1944; lieutenant, 1 November 1945; lieutenant commander, 1 March 1952; commander, 1 November 1956; captain, 1 July 1963.

From January to April 1943 he had operational training at the Naval Air Station, Miami, Florida, after which he served as navigator and gunnery officer of Fighting Squadron 31, based on the USS Cabot (CVL-28) and later on the USS Belleau Wood (CVL-24). As such he participated in all naval engagements from the Marshall Islands operation to the fall of the Japanese Empire. He was credited with shooting down 14 enemy aircraft, sinking various enemy ships, and assisting in the sinking of the Japanese battleship Ise.

For heroism and outstanding service during World War II, he was awarded the Navy Cross and gold stars in lieu of two additional awards; the Distinguished Flying Cross and gold stars in lieu of two additional awards; and the Air Medal with two gold stars. He is also entitled to wear the ribbon for the Navy Unit Commendation with star and facsimiles of the Presidential Unit Citations awarded the Cabot and Belleau Wood.

He was released to inactive duty status in October 1945, and upon his transfer to the U.S. Navy a year later, reported to the USS Portsmouth (CL-102). He served as senior aviator of that cruiser until May 1948. For 14 months thereafter he was attached to the naval air stations at Jacksonville, Florida, and Corpus Christi, Texas, assigned to the Blue Angels flight demonstration team. From July 1950 to August 1951 he served as executive officer of Fighter Squadron 191, based on the USS Princeton (CV-37), as the squadron participated in the Korean War. The Princeton was awarded the Navy Unit Commendation, and Hawkins personally was awarded a gold star in lieu of a fourth Air Medal for meritorious achievement during nine months of that period.

Returning to Corpus Christi in August 1951, he rejoined the Blue Angels and from 1952 to 1954 served as commanding officer of the flight team. When detached in April 1954 he reported to the General Line School, Monterey, California, where he was a student for six months. From October 1954 until September 1956 he was assigned as operations and projects officer of Experimental Squadron Five, attached first to the Naval Air Station, Moffett Field, California, later to the Naval Air Facility, China Lake, California. In September 1956 he reported to the Office of the Chief of Naval Operations, Navy Department, Washington, D.C., where he was technical adviser in the Progress Analysis Group during the making of films on various aspects of naval operations.

In March 1957 Hawkins assumed command of Attack Squadron 46 and from September 1958 to January 1960 served as air officer on board the USS Franklin D. Roosevelt (CVA-42). Following instruction at the Armed Forces Staff College, Norfolk,

Virginia, he assumed command in June 1960 of Carrier Air Group One. Assigned in August 1961 to the Office of the Chief of Naval Operations, he served as head of the Program Planning Division until July 1964 and the next month reported for instruction at the Naval War College, Newport, Rhode Island. In June 1965 he became commanding officer of the USS Caloosahatchee (AO-98) and in May 1966 was detached for duty in the Office of the Chief of Naval Operations, where he served as head of the Program Appraisal Division (OP-90E). In May of 1968 he was detached and assumed command of Naval Air Station Atsugi, Japan, where he served until August 1970. Returning to Washington, D.C., he assumed the position of Director, Community Relations for the Department of Defense and served in that billet until his retirement in June of 1973. After retirement from active duty, he became the secretary/treasurer and chief of staff of the Naval Aviation Museum Foundation. He has been instrumental in the development of the National Museum of Naval Aviation in Pensacola, Florida.

He was awarded the Navy Cross with two gold stars; the Distinguished Flying Cross with two gold stars, the Air Medal with three gold stars, the Presidential Unit Citation (two awards); the Navy Unit Commendation Ribbon; the Asiatic-Pacific Campaign Medal with 11 operations stars; American Campaign Medal; World War II Victory Medal; Navy Occupation Service Medal; China Service Medal (extended); National Defense Service Medal; Korean Service Medal with three stars; United Nations Service Medal; Korean Presidential Unit Citation; and the Navy Expert Pistol Shot medal. For his service to Japan during his tour of duty as commanding officer at Atsugi, Captain Hawkins was awarded the Third Order of the Sacred Treasure by the Emperor of Japan.

Captain Hawkins is married to the former Louise Bancroft of Mobile, Alabama. He has three children: Raymond Guy Hawkins, Michael Gregory Hawkins, and Jennifer Jill Hawkins.

Authorization

The U.S. Naval Institute is hereby authorized to make available to individuals, libraries, and other repositories of its choosing the transcripts of two oral history interviews concerning the life and career of the undersigned. The interviews were recorded on 14 and 15 July 1983 in collaboration with Paul Stillwell for the U.S. Naval Institute.

The undersigned does hereby release and assign to the U.S. Naval Institute all right, title, restrictions, and interest in the interviews. The copyright in both the oral and transcribed versions shall be the sole property of the U.S. Naval Institute. The tape recordings of the interviews are and will remain the property of the U.S. Naval Institute.

Signed and sealed this __13th__ day of __AUGUST__ 1996.

Arthur R. Hawkins
Arthur R. Hawkins, U.S. Navy (Retired)

Interview Number 1 with Captain Arthur R. Hawkins, U.S. Navy (Retired)

Place: Naval Aviation Museum, Pensacola, Florida

Date: Thursday, 14 July 1983

Interviewer: Paul Stillwell

Q: Captain, could you begin, please, by telling the circumstances that led you to join the Navy right after the beginning of World War II?

Captain Hawkins: At the time Pearl Harbor was bombed, I was at Lon Morris College in Jacksonville, Texas. I was on a basketball scholarship from the University of Texas. They farmed me out to the junior college for two years. While at Lon Morris, I had taken what was called CPT, civilian pilot training, and had received my pilot's license at the time.

My brother, who was a pilot in the Army Air Corps, was killed at Port Moresby during the early, early part of the war.* So I decided to leave college at that time and enter the service myself. I had my pilot's license already, and I wanted to get into aviation. Jacksonville, Texas, is very close to Dallas, which was the central recruiting area for the Navy flight program. I joined up in Dallas for the naval aviation cadet program right out of college.†

Q: How old were you at that point?

---

* His brother's name was Alva Guy Hawkins. Port Moresby is a seaport on the south coast of New Guinea, not far from Australia. On 20 June 1941 the U.S. Army Air Corps had been officially redesignated the U.S. Army Air Forces.
† In 1935 Congress instituted the aviation cadet program whereby individuals enlisted in the Naval Reserve, then were trained as aviators and sent to the fleet in cadet status until later being commissioned as officers. In 1939 the program was modified so that individuals were commissioned upon successful completion of flight training.

Captain Hawkins: At that point, in April 1942, I was 19 years old. By December I would have been 20, but at that time I was 19.

Then, after signing up in Dallas, I was called to aviation training. I took my E-base training in Dallas.* Finishing up in Dallas, we were transferred to Corpus Christi to finish our basic and advanced training. This was after about three months in Dallas. You had mostly your ground school and your solo there. Of course, in my case, and for several others who already had their pilots' licenses, we were able to advance past the solo phase and almost into formation flying by the time we did get out of there.

Q: What kind of planes were you flying?

Captain Hawkins: We were flying the NP-1, a Navy trainer which was built in Philly.† While we were there, the Navy bought a bunch of Piper Cubs, and they also brought in some Stearmans, which were designated N2Ss.‡ Now, in my case I had been flying the Waco in civilian pilot training, and it had a steerable tail wheel. The N2Ss the Navy bought at that time had steerable tail wheels, whereas the other Navy airplanes had locked or unlocked tail wheels. So for my initial training they put me into the Stearmans, since I had some experience with the steerable tail wheel already.

Q: Did that steerable tail wheel make a difference in how the plane handled? What was the advantage or disadvantage?

---

* E-base stood for elimination base, essentially a place to weed out those who did not show potential for the full flight training course.
† The Spartan NP-1 was a biplane trainer. It was 24 feet long, had a wing span of 34 feet, gross weight of 3,006 pounds, and a top speed of 108 miles per hour.
‡ The Stearman N2S Kaydet was a biplane trainer first ordered by the Army as the PT-13. It was 25 feet long, had a wing span of 32 feet, gross weight of 2,717 pounds, and a top speed of 124 miles per hour.

Captain Hawkins: Well, the big part of it was that if you were used to a locked tail wheel upon landing, you didn't have to worry too much about a ground loop. The plane wouldn't swerve from side to side while the tail wheel was locked. But your steerable tail wheels were hooked to the rudders, and they would come unlocked after you pushed the rudder, say, 20 degrees. The possibility of a ground loop was the main concern of the locked tail wheel over the non-locked tail wheel. Eventually, the Navy modified all the Stearmans so they had locked tail wheels.

Q: Why hadn't they been built that way in the first place if that was a problem?

Captain Hawkins: Well, as you know, for landing on a carrier a steerable tail wheel is not something you're going to need. You want a firm lock to come in aboard ship. That, basically, was the reason for the difference from the Army Air Corps version of the Stearman, which had a steerable, unlocked tail wheel.

Q: Were you put into a group of contemporaries that had about the same amount of previous training as you?

Captain Hawkins: Once you had reached the formation stage of training, you ended up with everybody in your group having about the same number of hours. Each instructor would be carrying about eight students, and that was after they had soloed and got into basic and so forth. He would have eight planes in his formation, and he would teach them formation flying. When you entered into your instrument training or something later, you'd go with one instructor one day, and maybe a different one the next day. But for formation, the same instructor carried you all the way through, as he did in primary. And to get you through solo, you had one instructor for that.

Q: What differences did you see in the Navy flying versus what you'd had before?

Captain Hawkins: Well, not too much. Actually, all we had done in civilian pilot work was to get our license and get our ten hours up to solo. Then we had started into our civilian basic training, where they started teaching you how to fly on instruments. For instruments in those days needle ball and airspeed were about all you had. But the Navy training had a set routine in primary; you got there and got your solo out of the way. Then in basic they would teach you all the basic skills of short-field landings, slips to circles, and all this stuff to give you confidence in the use of the airplane. Then you would go into advanced training, after you'd built up your skills in basic. In advanced training you went into a little hotter airplane, which was then the SNJ.[*] They would teach you formation, gunnery, bombing, and the combat maneuvers in the SNJ. Then you would leave.

Out of advanced training you would receive your commission as an ensign, and then they would send you to operational training. In operational training you would be flying a combat airplane of some sort. In my case that was the Brewster Buffalo.[†] These were the same type the Marines had on Wake Island, and some were returned to Miami. They were pretty beat-up airplanes. I mean, they'd been shot full of holes and this and that, but they were combat airplanes. We did our training in them in Miami and Opa-Locka, Florida.

Q: Did you have combat veterans as flight instructors?

---

[*] The SNJ Texan trainer, built by North American Aviation, first went into service in the late 1930s. Specifications for the SNJ-5 model included a length of 29 feet, 6 inches; wing span of 42 feet, gross weight of 5,300 pounds, and maximum speed of 205 miles per hour.
[†] The Brewster F2A Buffalo was the first monoplane fighter to enter Navy operational squadrons, which it did in mid-1941. The F2A-3 had a wing span of 35 feet, length of 26 feet, gross weight of 7,159 pounds, and top speed of 321 miles per hour. It was armed with four .50-caliber machine guns.

Captain Hawkins: There would be maybe one here and one there; every so often, somebody would come back. There just hadn't been much time for them to get back. I'd say by the time I reached the squadron, the first groups were coming back from combat. The Navy was then feeding them in as experienced people to bolster new squadrons as they were forming. But none had shown up at Miami when we were there. The men we learned from were basically the experienced naval aviators who had been in the field of aviation for a long time. They were veteran instructors, especially in operational, when you started your night work and that type of thing when you had very few hours of advanced training left.

Q: Were you getting reports back from the combat theaters on tactics and doctrine and so forth?

Captain Hawkins: Oh, yes, especially by the time we reached operational training. The Thach Weave, as it was called, was then coming into its own.* We were taught the Thach Weave in our fighter tactics of how to counter the maneuverability of the Japanese Zero--the best ways to do this, best ways to do that.†

Q: What was your commissioning date?

Captain Hawkins: I was commissioned the first day of January 1943. So you can see it was pretty speedy in those days. I went into the Navy in April and finished my training through advanced by the first day of the following year.

---

* The Thach Weave was developed by Lieutenant Commander John S. Thach, USN, commanding officer of Fighting Squadron Three, as a means of enabling the F4F Wildcat to counter the better-performing Japanese Zero fighter. Thach, who retired as a four-star admiral, described the origin of the maneuver in his Naval Institute oral history.
† The Mitsubishi-built A6M Zero was the best-known fighter plane in the Japanese Navy in World War II. The standard A6M2 had a top speed of 317 miles per hour and was armed with two 7.7-millimeter machine guns and two 20-millimeter cannons.

Q: Please describe the operational training. Did you have mock dogfights? What sort of things went on?

Captain Hawkins: Well, in advanced training you got all the maneuvers of gunnery runs and bombing runs and so forth, but you had been able to drop only miniature bombs. And the SNJ's little single gun was not much to bring you into actual combat. In operational training you actually fired .50-caliber guns. The Brewster had two guns in the wings, but we used only the two in the cowling. They fired through the prop, a synchronized prop. We did a lot of gunnery on towed sleeves. We did a lot of bombing on control targets. We did a lot of formation work in four-man teams. That was the basic unit of the formation, a four-plane unit operating together. In operational training they taught you the Thach Weave, how to protect each other, and this type of thing.

Q: Did you ever have anything taught then, such as the Thach Weave, that you directly applied in combat?

Captain Hawkins: Oh, certainly. The Thach Weave certainly applied in combat, from the minute you started until you completed. I mean, it was a matter of knowing that your enemy could out-turn you and outmaneuver you, so you set yourself up to counteract him. You used the characteristics of the airplane that you knew you could do better than he could, such as the dive and turn, to get away from him at high speed. With the Thach Weave you always had somebody turning into the enemy plane at the same time he was turning into the tail of your wingman. As you weaved back and forth, you always had two guns from the section pointing at the direction the enemy was coming from. So it certainly applied all during that. And, of course, your bombing was something you had to learn in operational, and that was certainly an asset when you finally got to combat.

Q: What kinds of targets? You said it was a control target. What did that entail?

Captain Hawkins: Control targets were manned by individuals who would tell you where your bomb hit. You'd be able to know, "Okay, I hit at 2:00 o'clock at 200 feet," or "I hit at 3:00 o'clock at 500 feet," or whatever it might be. It gave you some indication of sighting and the use of your sight for the bombing.

Q: Were these water-filled bombs?

Captain Hawkins: We used the water-filled a lot for the actual feeling of, say, a 250-pounder. Your water-fills were usually about 100-pound size. We mostly used the little smoke practice bombs--Mark 8, I think they were called. It was about an 8- to 12-pound bomb with a cartridge in the back that would pop smoke when it hit the ground. That would give you a marking of where your bomb actually hit.

After operational, they then sent you for carquals.* You went either to Norfolk or up in the Great Lakes. In my case I went to Norfolk on the USS Charger, which was more or less an operational-type carrier.† I did my 12 carrier landings in an SNJ.

Q: What was it like to land on a ship that small?

Captain Hawkins: I landed on CVLs the whole war, so it didn't bother me at all.‡ I didn't know any better; when I got there, I thought that was big.

---

* Carquals--qualification landings and takeoffs on an aircraft carrier.
† The USS Charger was classified ACV-30, an auxiliary aircraft carrier, on 20 August 1942. She was reclassified CVE-30, an escort aircraft carrier, on 15 July 1943. She was 492 feet long; 69 feet, 6 inches in the beam; and displaced 8,000 tons.
‡ CVLs were light aircraft carriers, built on hulls originally intended for light cruisers. Those of the Independence (CVL-22) class were 622 feet long, 72 feet in the beam, and displaced 11,000 tons.

Q: Had you had any practice landings on fields that size ashore to get you prepared?

Captain Hawkins: Oh, yes. The carrier qualifications on land were controlled. You had the carrier deck marked out. In those days your LSO, which was all we had working with us on land, would bring you right on in to a runway marked off with the size of the deck you would be using for your carquals.* The FCLPs would go 5, 10, 12 hops before you were turned loose on the carrier.† Then, after you had qualified on board ship, you reported to your squadron.

Q: Please describe your first landing on the Charger.

Captain Hawkins: Well, the landing doesn't stick in my mind as much as the weather. The ship was off outside the Chesapeake Bay, which was too confined to operate in. The weather around Norfolk was so miserable that I think it took three days of going out and coming in before we could get our 12 landings in. But the carrier landings became routine after a while.

I'm sure there was that moment of fear when I was coming up the groove to catch the wire for the first time.‡ But the weather was more a concern; I still remember thinking I wasn't going to get it done in time to get to my squadron. Actually, it was strictly a case of making the landings and getting them over with and gone, because certainly you didn't become a part of the ship or anything else under this. You went out, and you never did go below deck on the carrier. You did your landings, and they sent you home. So you really didn't learn the feel of a ship and so forth, because it was all done from land. You came out, got in the pattern, did five or six, back to the beach and refueled, and came back and

---

* LSO--landing signal officer.
† FCLP--field carrier landing practice.
‡ When a plane comes in on an aircraft carrier's deck, it is stopped by catching an arresting wire with a tailhook that hangs down from the bottom of the fuselage.

did five or six more. So everything you saw during your quals was what went on on deck, which is the essential thing anyway.

Q: How many people that you started out with were thrown by the wayside as all this went on?

Captain Hawkins: Oh, I imagine the attrition rate was around 20%. Either they fell by in ground school, or they fell by in basic advanced primary training when they couldn't solo. Then, when they got to advanced, the big drop was usually the carquals. By the time you got through operational, you should be seasoned enough to do it, but the carquals were pretty tough for some people.

Of course, aviators were hard to come by in those days, and they needed them. They didn't wash anybody out and send them home. When the pilots had reached that stage, they already had their wings, so if they couldn't carqual, they just went into transports or some other type of flying.

Q: How much of a screening process was there? Twenty percent seems low to me, as if there was a fairly careful selection of who would undertake this training.

Captain Hawkins: Well, certainly the physical and mental requirements were quite strenuous. In order to enter you had your psychological tests as well as your mechanical. And your physical was very, very strenuous. In my case, back when I was six years old I'd had diphtheria, and I had had a tracheotomy at that age. I was held up for a couple of months on my physical until I got certification from the doctor who had performed that tracheotomy that I had no ill effect from it. So I was able to come in on it at that time, after his certification. Thank gosh he hadn't died or something; he was still around.

The requirements were very, very strict. Maybe they got a little less later, when they needed more pilots, more pilots, more pilots. But that was right at the initial part, the buildup of naval aviation, so it was still very strict. Lots and lots of people would drop out on their initial written exams. You didn't understand some of the questions, but they were there. The grading system, as I understood it, your scores on your mechanical had to do with the grading on your aptitude.

They might ask you, "Would you like to jump over a cliff with a knife in your mouth to fight alligators?" If somebody said "Yes," he missed it. It's hard to figure out.

Q: Was that part of the psychological testing?

Captain Hawkins: Yes, the psychological testing. One of the questions they asked you was, "How old was your mother when you were born?" And I do know that one guy said his mother was 19 when he was born, and he missed that question. That was bumped against maybe he'd made a 98 in his math and a 74 in his English, and these things were correlated together. They used this particular gauge to grade his psychological tests, and in that question his mother should have been older. That's basically the way it was figured out.

Q: Was this to separate people who were perhaps too high-strung?

Captain Hawkins: Basically they had, at that time, figured the type of individual they wanted or needed for an aviator, I guess. That test was structured around that type of questions. So that, basically, is about as far as it went.

Q: And you were considered normal.

Captain Hawkins: I made it, anyway. I got by that part.

Q: Was your athletic background taken into account?

Captain Hawkins: Well, not necessarily. Your physical well-being was. Certainly you had to be at least 5 feet, 4 inches. You couldn't be 6 feet, 5 inches, or 6 feet 4½, I think it was. Your weight was a big factor--I mean, on your frame. You had to fall on the charts within the frame of your physique. Blood pressure was a factor. For eyes it was either 20/20 or nothing--no correction at all. Teeth were a big factor in your physical in those days because of the oxygen systems. You couldn't have an overbite or an underbite. They hadn't corrected it to the fact that they used to hang an oxygen tube in there and suck on it. Your overbite would bite that in two. By then we already had oxygen masks, and they should have changed that requirement, but it stayed with them for years--no overbite. They were trying for a certain type of individual, certainly one physically capable of handling it.

Q: Admiral Radford was in charge of flight training and set up a preflight program that was very heavy on athletics.* Did that come along later than when you went through?

Captain Hawkins: That was later, yes. Actually, the preflight was to build up a pool, because it came to the point where you needed a flow of aviators going through. Some were being lost, and the new airplanes were being built--new squadrons, new air groups, and so forth. So, basically, preflight built this pool and weeded out early--before they even got to the training of actually flying--those individuals that they thought couldn't hack it. So they had ground school and an awful lot of athletics. In preflight you usually got about ten hours of flying. If you got through that, then you went on to primary training. But that was later. When preflight started, you had to go through that first, then you'd go to E-base, then to primary training, basic training, and on through.

---

* Captain Arthur W. Radford, USN, Director of Aviation Training, Bureau of Aeronautics, 1942-43. Radford, later a four-star admiral, served as Chairman of the Joint Chiefs of Staff in the mid-1950s.

Arthur R. Hawkins #1 - 12

Q: When you were coming up, they were bringing out not only the CVLs, but the Essex class was building up also, so they needed a lot of people.*

Captain Hawkins: That's right.

Q: And perhaps cut the program short for that reason.

Captain Hawkins: Yes. In fact, all they had at that time were the E-bases. The preflight had not even started. In fact, the preflight actually sent them up to colleges where they reported. And that way they had a pool that could keep the pipeline full at all times. So that worked out good. But, when the war was over, that pipeline was too full. They had an awful lot of people who would have liked to come on through and get their training. But they were not able to, because the Navy had to weed them out. Then the qualifications got so high that very few could meet them.

Q: After your carquals you reported to your squadron.

Captain Hawkins: I reported to my squadron. It was Fighter Squadron 31, VF-31, in Air Group 31. It was to be formed up in Atlantic City, New Jersey, which was a brand-new air station.

Q: When did you report to that squadron?

Captain Hawkins: I reported to that squadron in about April or May of '43--somewhere in there. Ten ensigns showed up in Atlantic City. They were still building the station. They

---

* The USS Essex (CV-9) was commissioned 31 December 1942 and was soon joined by a number of sister ships that greatly increased the Navy's aircraft carrier capability. These ships were each 872 feet long, had a beam of 93 feet, top speed of 33 knots, and displaced 34,881 tons at full load.

didn't have the runways finished, and there were no airplanes on board. So we had to go to Philadelphia to get our flight time in while they were finishing the field. Naturally, the ten ensign aviators that had shown up for VF-31 were assigned duties as BOQ officers, to see that the BOQ got built and built right.* We were also mess officers and this, that, and the other--until our commanding officer reported aboard.

The hangars slowly got finished, and the field got finished. Then we started bringing our airplanes in. We went to Norfolk, picked them up, and flew them in. We flew them into the little old civilian field in Atlantic City first. Then they finished one runway, and we were able to start training at the Atlantic City Naval Air Station. Actually we were a CVL air group, which at that time was composed of 12 fighters, F6Fs; 12 SBDs, the bombing group; and 12 TBFs, the torpedo group. We were the air group assigned to the Cabot, which was being built in Philly.†

During our training, they had changed the composition of the CVL air group to 24 F6Fs and 12 TBFs; they had dropped the SBDs. They took our SBD squadron, as they did a lot of other SBD squadrons, and sent them on out to Guadalcanal.‡ They operated off the beaches out there in support of Guadalcanal. We completed our training in Atlantic City, and the Cabot was completed. As she came down the river from Philly, we picked her up and trained with her in the Atlantic.

Q: When did you first get aboard the ship?

Captain Hawkins: Let me look in my logbook here, and I'll see. We went aboard the Cabot on 1 September '43.

---

* BOQ--bachelor officers' quarters.
† The USS Cabot (CVL-28) was built by the New York Shipbuilding Company, Camden, New Jersey, across the Delaware River from Philadelphia. She was commissioned 24 July 1943 at the Philadelphia Navy Yard.
‡ U.S. forces invaded the island of Guadalcanal in the South Pacific on 7 August 1942 and subsequently operated Douglas SBD dive-bombers and other planes from the Henderson Field airstrip on the island.

Q: Who was the commanding officer of your squadron?

Captain Hawkins: The squadron commander was R. A. Winston.* He was the naval aviator who had written the book Dive Bomber and a couple of others. The air group commander was Lieutenant Commander Vredenburgh.† As it turned out, by the time we actually deployed they had changed the composition of the air group. Winston became the air group commander later, after Vredenburgh left, because he had the 24-plane squadron. In that case he was usually the CAG as well as the fighter squadron commander.‡

You asked the question about combat veterans showing up. We had about four who had returned from the Pacific to join our squadron. They were lieutenant (junior grades). So the squadron ended up with a composition of a lieutenant commander for a skipper, a couple of lieutenants, about six or seven jaygees, and the rest ensigns.§

Q: Winston was probably learning from some of his subordinates what it was like out there.

Captain Hawkins: That's true, very true, because he had not been out.

Q: How was he as a pilot and a leader?

---

* Lieutenant Commander Robert A. Winston, USN. His books were as follows: Dive Bomber (New York: Holiday House, 1939); Aces Wild (New York: Holiday House, 1941); Aircraft Carrier (New York: Harper & Brothers, 1942); Fighting Squadron (New York: Holiday House, 1946). The latter is an account of his World War II experiences, including command of VF-31.
† Lieutenant Commander James B. Vredenburgh III, USN.
‡ CAG--commander carrier air group. A carrier air group comprised all the planes assigned to the ship. The air group commander was the senior pilot in a flying billet, as opposed to being part of ship's company.
§ Jaygee--lieutenant (junior grade).

Captain Hawkins: Very good. He was a leader as far as joining the group together and following the routine that should be established and the training. You can see with that many young, young ensigns you've got a real green group to get going. But with the time limits we were working under, you either got it in a hurry, or you didn't make the grade. Because the ship went through the Panama Canal in November and headed around to the Pacific side. My logbook shows that we arrived at Kaneohe in the Hawaiian Islands at the end of November.*

Q: Can you describe the comparison in operating from that CVL class and from the Essex class?

Captain Hawkins: Well, at that time I had not operated from an Essex-class carrier, so to me it was routine. The only actual difference was that the deck was much narrower. You had to be lined up coming in. There was no way to be off-center and make your landing. The length had nothing to do with it, since your landing area was about the same length as the landing area on an Essex-class carrier. But the width of the Essex was certainly much greater because the CVL had been built on a cruiser hull.

With all that flight deck on top of it, the Cabot had a tendency to roll much more than the Essex class. So in rough seas you were fighting a pitching and rolling deck. Certainly our ship's acceleration was greater than the Essex, being on that clean-cut cruiser hull and having the cruiser engines still in it. She was good for 32-33 knots quickly. I mean, it would come up to speed much faster than the wide-bottomed Essex class.

---

* Kaneohe was the site of a naval air station on the eastern side of Oahu, Hawaii. The ship moored at Pearl Harbor on 27 November, and the air group flew to the air station. For details on the ship's operations in World War II, see J. Ed Hudson, The History of the USS Cabot (CVL 28): A Fast Carrier in World War II (Privately published; a copy is in the Naval Institute reference library.)

The operations were different in that, being a small unit, the air group people knew the shipboard people. On the Essex you could be there for a year and not know who the first lieutenant was. In our case, being a smaller ship with a smaller crew, it just seemed that you knew you were in more of a family-type affair than aboard the larger ships. And the camaraderie was much better, I thought, than it was on the Essex class. Other than that, a CVL pilot was always a CVL pilot and proud of it.

Q: Was there a little feeling that you could do a tougher job because of that?

Captain Hawkins: Oh, certainly. When a CVL pilot would land over on an Essex-class carrier, he'd ask which runway to use. Just to put the needle into them, you know: "Right or left runway? Which one?"

Q: Any difference when you got in the air? The planes were all the same then.

Captain Hawkins: Probably enough, yes. Of course, in our case the Cabot was in combat out there for almost ten months, so we became the air group with the most combat experience. It kind of hurt the big CV groups that would show up; we got all the gravy hops because we were the senior group out there. When fighter sweeps came up, we would usually end up with them. The other air groups would end up protecting the bombers, flying close control, or whatever. But that was something that you earned with the seniority of being there the longest, being the most experienced. When the admiral wanted a fighter sweep in the latter part of our tour, usually we got it. After we had been in combat for so long, it was sort of old hat.

Q: You said you were close to the people in the ship's company. Do you remember any of those particularly?

Captain Hawkins: Oh, sure. In those days you had a lot of well-known names. One of our CIC officers was Marshall Field.* Our ship's athletic officer was Langhurst, the all-American tackle from Michigan State or Michigan.† Zimmerman was understudy for Tommy Harmon back in those days when Tommy was the big gun for the quarterbacks. He was a pilot on board the ship.‡

And you talk about those prisoner of war hops that we mentioned earlier, before we started taping, we had a man who was in Time magazine or Life magazine. He was the one that bet he could make a hole in one on a 210-yard hole if he played from sunup to sundown. I believe his name was Hughes, and he was a CIC officer, an intelligence officer. He took one of the prisoner of war hops in the back of one of our TBFs.§ The TBF spun in over the POW camp, and they all ended up in the camp over there.

We had all kinds of people like that. We had a champion diver from the Olympics. I forget his name. But we were all very close. In fact, the air group would play the ship in volleyball and whatever you could play on board ship. Camaraderie and close competition were going on all the time. It didn't happen too much on the Essex class, because it was just too huge. Their air group was much larger than ours.

Q: Who was your ship's skipper?

Captain Hawkins: Well, let's see. To start out we had Schoeffel.** Then, for most of the

---

* Lieutenant (junior grade) Marshall Field, Jr., USNR, was part of the family that ran the Marshall Field department store in Chicago.
† Lieutenant (junior grade) E. J. Langhurst, USNR.
‡ Lieutenant (junior grade) R. O. Zimmerman, USNR. Tom Harmon of the University of Michigan was college football's Heisman Trophy winner in 1940.
§ The Grumman-built TBF Avenger was the U.S. Navy's standard carrier-based torpedo plane during the latter part of World War II.
** Captain Malcolm F. Schoeffel, USN, commanded the USS Cabot (CVL-28) from 24 July 1943 to 5 May 1944. His oral history is in the Naval Institute collection.

time out in the Pacific, it was Captain Michael.* Over on the Belleau Wood, which I went to later in the war, they had Air Medal Tomlinson.† We called him that because that was the biggest medal he'd pass out. He wouldn't give you anything else.

Q: How soon did you get into combat?

Captain Hawkins: Well, our first campaign was the Marshalls, which began with our carrier strikes in the latter part of January of '44. We supported the landings on Kwajalein on the first day of February. On February 16 we went over and hit Truk so no fleet could come out of there to disrupt the landings going on. During the Marshalls our group shot down five Zeros. I wasn't lucky enough to get a score during that time.

Q: What do you remember about your first combat hop?

Captain Hawkins: Well, my first combat hop actually started out easy. The CAP, which was the combat air patrol, would fly over the ships. We started flying combat air patrol on the way to the Marshalls. These were considered combat hops because the Japanese planes might come out to meet you. My first combat hop, as such, was supporting the landings going ashore at Kwajalein. With an F6F they could put 250- or 500-pound bombs on.‡ So during the landings we would be loaded with 500-pounders and go in and drop them, then strafe as necessary. I can remember very well during the landings when a

---

* Captain Stanley J. Michael, USN, commanded the USS Cabot (CVL-28) from 5 May 1944 to 6 February 1945.
† Captain William G. Tomlinson, USN, commanded the USS Belleau Wood (CVL-24), a sister ship of the Cabot, from 26 January 1945 to 15 December 1945.
‡ Grumman F6F Hellcat fighters first entered fleet squadrons in early 1943. The model used in this operation was the F6F-3, which was 33 feet, 7 inches long; wing span of 42, feet 10 inches; gross weight of 12,415 pounds; and top speed of 388 miles per hour. It was armed with six .50-caliber machine guns.

big battleship was sitting off and lobbing in these big old shells. You could actually see the shells. You'd watch them all the way in until they hit.

One of the news correspondents was killed during this raid, I remember. They thought it was one of these shells that hit the airplane, because the airplane that he was in disappeared. The assumption was that maybe one of those 16-inch shells and the airplane had joined up together. Anyhow, that was my first hop. I remember dropping the bombs and strafing, assisting the troops on shore, and then covering them while they were going in. So hit here, hit there. We'd assist them under our grid system as we were using then. We supported the complete landings until the troops were ashore and what they call secure. Then the fleet shoved off to hit Truk.*

Q: I have read that there was a great deal of apprehension going in. That was supposedly the impregnable bastion.

Captain Hawkins: That's right. We'd never gone that far over, you know, and also we were hoping to catch more ships in there than we did. They probably knew we were coming. But an awful lot of damage was done in that area. But it was just to hit and get out, just to tear it up so that no fleet would come out and try to disrupt the landings going on in Kwajalein.

Q: What was your role in that attack?

Captain Hawkins: I took in a 1,000-pound bomb on that strike. Let's see, it's right here. We had a bombing flight. Actually we took in bombs to pit the airfield. They were set for 2 hours, 4 hours, 9 hours, 12 hours, you know, just various time fuzes on these bombs. We would take them in and stick them in the runway. Then they would go off, just to

---

* For details see Barrett Tillman, "Hellcats Over Truk," U.S. Naval Institute Proceedings, March 1977, pages 63-71.

keep the field from being used, so no planes could come out of it. In my case, on the 16th of February I had a 1,000-pound bomb with a six-hour delay, and I dropped it on the airfield at Truk.

Q: How did it affect the handling characteristics of the airplane to have a good-sized bomb on it?

Captain Hawkins: It was just sluggish; that's all. Ordinarily the F6F would have a belly tank down under there anyway. So you had 150 gallons of gas at eight pounds a gallon. You'd take that off and stick a 2,000-pound bomb as max. In this particular case it was a 1,000-pound bomb. We hit Truk, and then as we came back, we took swipes at Woleai Island and Palau, just hitting anything and everything as we came back. We were just covering them to be sure that nothing came out to bother the landings that were going on.

Q: When did you get into your first air-to-air combat?

Captain Hawkins: Well, my division was made up of four airplanes, and the first kill in our division was made on April 1. A kid named Hayde, who was number-four man in our division, shot down a Betty.* We were on CAP, and we all shot at it, but Hayde got credit for it. He flamed it, and down she went. My first kill came on April 29, during our second raid on Truk. I was on standby. You go on various stages of standby because of feasibility and closeness of a raid or what have you.

In this particular case we were in the cockpits on a catapult, our standby position. A raid of 12 torpedo bombers came in from Truk to hit the ships coming in. The planes were low on the water, and they didn't pick them up until they were about 15 miles out. So they turned us up and launched us. I was on the starboard cat, and they launched. As

---

* Lieutenant (junior grade) Frank F. Hayde, Jr., USNR. "Betty" was the Allied code name for the Japanese Navy's Mitsubishi G4M land-based medium bomber.

they launched me, the ships opened up with their guns at these 12 torpedo planes. As I went off the cat, I turned into the flight coming in, and then I was head-to-head with a Judy.* So I opened up on him and splashed him there, then pulled up in sort of a quick chandelle, getting my gear up and what have you.† Then I turned and followed the remainder on through the force while these 18 destroyers, two cruisers, two battleships, and three carriers were firing at these planes coming through.

Q: A little hairy, was it?

Captain Hawkins: Well, it was one flight I'll always remember; let's put it that way. But I did get through; I didn't get hit. Luckily enough, I was over them. I was a little higher than they were. They were right on the water, dropping their fish at the ships, and everybody was shooting. We had a few ships shoot up each other in this particular case. I followed them all the way through the force, out the other side. The kid who went off the other cat had turned and gone back through. Then I joined with him on the other side, and we pursued them under radar control. He got one more of the planes that went in.

Q: Did that experience do a good deal to build your confidence at that point?

Captain Hawkins: Oh, yes. It was about time I ended up with something. Of course, just following that is when the big "Turkey Shoot" came about.‡ As you know, the Jap fleet was coming across at us. Their plan was to launch from their carriers way out, hit our ships, and then go on into Guam and land. That particular day I was with my division on a

---

* "Judy" was the Allied code name for the Japanese Navy's D4Y carrier-based dive-bomber.
† A chandelle is an abrupt climbing turn by an airplane in which the momentum of the plane is used to gain a higher rate of climb.
‡ The "Great Marianas Turkey Shoot" took place on 19 June 1944 while U.S. carriers were supporting the invasion of Saipan. That day U.S. planes shot down more than 300 Japanese aircraft.

combat air patrol at 25,000 feet, sitting there waiting for them to come. The first wave that hit the ships were fighters; they came in ahead, with the big fighter-bombers coming in later. So it must have been a good flight of 40 or 50 that came in in the first wave of mostly fighters. There were some Judys, some bombers, with them but not very many in the first wave.

Our division was vectored out to hit on that first wave. And we were in perfect position about 3,000-4,000 feet above them. As they came in, we dove into them from above. My division accounted for 13 airplanes on that particular hop. I got three. Everybody got three, except one guy, Wirth, who got four; he was one of the combat veterans from before.[*] They hit us with three waves that day. Actually, it was so timed that when we finished and were getting low on fuel, we could not land back on our own ship. I landed on the Monterey that day, and so did the rest of my flight.[†] They refueled us, replenished us, re-ammoed us, and back in the air we went as soon as they could get back into the wind and launch again.

We were climbing back out. By that time, the last wave had come through. Of course, the ships had launched all the planes they could get into the air; they cleared the decks. They had launched bombers, everything. They had sent all the bombers over to orbit out near Guam, just to get them out of the way and leave the decks clear for the fighters to be able to cycle through the decks while this was going on. They had fighters over protecting the bombers as they were circling. Well, all the Japanese planes that had lived through the dogfights headed over to Guam to land. Well, some fighters were over there protecting our bombers that were out in that area. Here came all these Japanese planes into the Guam airfield to land. They were low on fuel, low on everything, and they were in a traffic pattern. I think one guy got about six or seven that day in the traffic pattern. It was a bad day at Black Rock for the Japanese that day.

---

[*] Lieutenant (junior grade) John L. Wirth, USN, a former enlisted pilot.
[†] The USS Monterey (CVL-26) was a sister ship of the Cabot.

Q: Why do you think it was so one-sided?

Captain Hawkins: Well, it was a desperate attempt to start with. We were in the middle, Guam on one side, and the Jap fleet had to come over us into Guam. They had launched at max range, wanting to keep their ships away from us, and they figured they could do it because they had a field to land on to refuel. Well, their communications were not too good, because we were getting ready to land on Guam. We had just beaten the hell out of it with bombs, strafing, and everything, and it just was not a good plan.

That particular day the weather was such that contrails were being formed at 20,000 feet. For some reason you usually don't see them down that low. You've got to get a little higher for contrails to form. Radar was just not needed that day; you'd see a flight coming in from 30 miles away because they were leaving contrails. And you've never seen anything like the dogfights going on over the ships. It was just a maze of contrails. So that hurt them too. No surprise at all. Also, they had to come in high because of conserving fuel the best they could. Radar was able to pick them up. We were ready for them; that's basically what it amounted to.

That particular night, we were taking aboard planes coming back in a little late. One of the Japanese airplanes got into the landing pattern of one of our ships and wanted to land aboard. It came all the way up to cut before they realized it was a Zero. He didn't land. He went off to land in the water somewhere, I guess, but he didn't come aboard. But it was just a very, very poorly planned endeavor. They weren't short of airplanes till then, but they were after that. It was that kind of a turkey shoot, really that bad.

Q: The Thach Weave had been devised because the F4F was really an inferior airplane to the Zero;. How was the comparison when you had the much better F6F?

Captain Hawkins: The F6F still could not outmaneuver the Zero. There were a lot of things you could do. You could dive and sharp turn left, and he couldn't follow you. I mean, if you were working high and he was on your tail, there was a way to shake him off. But you had a big advantage in terms of firepower and the survivability of the pilot and your airplane, for that matter. You had armor plate where he did not. You could take multiple hits from him and still operate, whereas one .50-caliber hit into his tank or into his flammable area, and he was done for. They had no self-sealing tanks, and they had no armor plate around the pilot. They'd done that to lighten the airplane so it would be maneuverable.

Q: Had your training emphasized what to aim at on the plane?

Captain Hawkins: Oh, yes. Oh, yes. By then they had picked up a couple of Zeros and had been testing them back in the States. The information was out on them and what you could do to best them. Mainly, you just had a better airplane, period. I mean, the plane could take multiple hits. If he didn't hit you, the airplane would still function. Emergency systems of all types were built into the airplane: self-sealing tanks, multiple systems for the control surfaces, two wires instead of one, non-flammable hydraulic fluid. And with the F6F, the Zero was not faster. You could finally outrun him if you got to diving away from him; you could leave him. Other than that, he still had a much more maneuverable airplane.

Q: Describe, in making an approach, how you went about shooting down a Zero.

Captain Hawkins: Well, actually the one I remember most, I guess, was one when I got in a tangled affair over Los Negros in the Philippines.

Q: This would have been in the fall of 1944, right?

Captain Hawkins: Yes, this was after we had moved on, and we had already hit Mindanao and the big island.* We had finished off on that and moved on up to the next group, which is where Los Negros is. There were four fields in the area controlled by the Japanese at that time. We went in as control close air support for the bombers. We were going in to bomb those four fields and try to put them out of whack while we were doing our business in there. We were flying right on the lower part of the formation, right with the bombers.

As we approached the field with our large flight of bombers, two Oscars made a pass on the formation.† They came right through the formation, firing as they went through. They didn't hit any of our bombers. But in support you couldn't get them, because they were coming straight down and went right through the force. With us on the low cover for the bombers, the air group commander called my flight leader, whose name was Stewart, and released him.‡ He said, "Go get them, Stew." So the four of us did a split-S and followed the two Oscars down to the ground. We caught one of them. We lost the other one in a dive; we don't know where he went.

I was able to get in position on the first one and come on in, straight down, and I hit him with all six of the .50-calibers going at him. It just thrust him in the ground. It was just like pushing, and down he went. As we pulled out from this dive on chasing these two airplanes, we were right over these four fields. Other planes were taking off with the four of us down there. So we pulled straight up to get a little altitude, and then we started picking these guys off as they were coming out. I had gotten a couple and, of course, the flight had picked up about three or four more. They stopped coming off the field, so we pulled up. We were sitting there waiting for them to get going again and not paying too much attention, you know.

---

* Hawkins is here recalling the events of 13 September 1944, during which he shot down five Japanese Oscars.
† The Nakajima-built Ki 43 Hayabusa (Falcon) was known by the Allied code name "Oscar." It was a fighter plane similar to the A6M Zero in appearance. The standard Ki 43 had a top speed of 320 miles per hour and was armed with two 12.7-millimeter machine guns.
‡ Lieutenant James S. Stewart, USN.

You've got to keep your six covered, and we forgot about that, because it was so much fun down below there.* So, for some reason or other, I was sitting there, looking down and waiting for somebody to get brave enough to start off again. I had a feeling there was something over here, so I looked, and there sat an Oscar in a perfect position to make a high-side run on me. In the old gunnery runs, you used to make runs on the sleeves. You'd set yourself up front, and you were in perfect position. I'll never forget that Oscar. He had the markings of the Marine squadron, which was their famous group. And it was just a beautiful airplane. Boy, it was shining. The thing was polished up so much that it made the Blue Angel airplanes of today look like dirt.† And I just thought, "Well, I am sitting here alone." My partner was on the other side, but if he had seen this plane at the same time I did, then we could have done the Thach Weave and started protecting ourselves.

Q: So your wingman wasn't with you?

Captain Hawkins: Here was the field, and he was on the other side. We were just looking down in here, and then I looked up, and there sat this bird up to my left. My first instinct was just to turn into him, even though I knew he could outmaneuver me. So I got the jump on him. When I turned, then here he came, but it was too late because I had already started my turn, which gave me the edge on him. As we pulled into each other, I was shooting with my firepower, and he just flew into it. We did the turn to come back, and he torched up here and just went off. So I'll always remember it, because in that particular case I did out-turn him in the F6F because I got the jump on him. So the old F6F was just a bird that was needed for the job.

---

* Keeping your six covered is a slang term for paying attention to the area right behind the plane--that is, the 6:00 o'clock position.
† The Blue Angels are members of the Navy's precision flight-demonstration team. Hawkins had two tours of duty with the Blue Angels during his career.

In fact, at the time the F6F had shown up, they were working on the F8F.* The F8F would have been better than the F6F for dogfighting the Zeros--much better. I mean, you could have out-done the Japanese in everything, but the Bearcat didn't have the other attributes that you needed during that time. It couldn't carry the bomb load that the F6F could carry, and the F6F could stay in the air much longer than the F8F. So they stuck with the F6F, and it was a good choice. After we got the upper hand, we never went on a flight that we wouldn't carry bombs. We'd carry bombs and drop them; then we were fighters. So the F6F was a wise choice for the mainstay airplane for World War II carriers.

Q: In a situation like that, did you have time to get scared, or did your instincts just take over?

Captain Hawkins: Well, I think probably you got more scared later, when you were thinking about it, than you were when it was happening. When you were in a melee or a dogfight, there was fear, yes. But that just charged up your adrenaline, and you were operating and functioning much better than you would have been if you didn't have a little fear. That's the way I figured it. It was seldom that you ended up part of a superior force. Lots of times on the Bonin Islands operation four of us would jump into 12 and things like that.† You think, "Man, I'm really going to have to stay with this to survive," although it turned out on your initial run at them you tried to wipe out enough to bring it back even again. But fear was there, certainly. Most of the fear, though, was when you got back to the ship and started thinking about it, reliving it. A fighter pilot had to feel like he was quail hunting or something, or he'd never function: "Get him, or he's going to get me."

---

* The F8F Bearcat was another Grumman-built Navy fighter plane. The XF8F-1 prototype first flew in August 1944, and the Bearcat first joined an operational squadron in May 1945.
† The fast carriers struck the Bonin Islands in August 1944. Shot down over one of the Bonins, Chichi Jima, on 2 September was Ensign George Bush, USNR. He was in the air group from the San Jacinto (CVL-30), a sister ship of the Cabot.

Once you're into it, you don't think about the possibility that he's going to get you. You're going to get him; that's it.

Q: And, of course, we don't know the feelings of the people who wound up not making it.

Captain Hawkins: That's true--very, very true.

Q: Was that the operation in which you became an ace?

Captain Hawkins: No, I had become an ace on 8 July 1944, during the raids on Iwo Jima.[*]

Q: How many did you wind up with?

Captain Hawkins: Five that day. I went out with 14 altogether. These were during our long first tour out there, which lasted almost a year.[†] When we went back, there just wasn't anything to shoot at, so to speak. I shot up at least 59 planes when they were on the ground. We were on bombing sweeps. We'd go in and drop our bombs; then we'd just sit around and shoot at the planes on the ground. They just didn't get them in the air the latter part of the war, although the kamikazes were running over everybody. They were waiting to protect the fatherland, I guess. They were saving all their good stuff, because they knew we were coming.

---

[*] A fighter pilot qualifies as an ace by shooting down five enemy airplanes.
[†] The Cabot was part of the deployed fast carrier task force from January 1944 to April 1945. Air Group 29 relieved Air Group 31, of which Hawkins was a member, on 5 October 1944 at Ulithi Atoll and remained on board until 28 April 1945.

Q: Speaking in general of your combat tours, how useful to you were the CIC fighter director officers?[*]

Captain Hawkins: Couldn't have done it without them as far as CAP went, you know. Most of them during that time, as you probably know, were reserve officers.[†] They were shoe salesmen or whatever they'd come from. We had some crackerjacks. They had learned their equipment, and, of course, it wasn't sophisticated equipment like nowadays. But by knowing his equipment the FDO was able to give you a halfway decent altitude, which he could tell by when the contact faded in and out. The radar itself didn't tell you altitude in those days. Those fighter directors were good; there's no doubt about it. They'd put you onto those birds coming in.

Of course, something you could never understand was what the Japanese were thinking. They'd send a single plane out. If he didn't make it back, they knew the fleet was out there. That's basically the way it must have been, because you'd get that day after day. They'd send out one airplane to scout the fleet, and we'd shoot him down. But they'd do it again the next day.

Q: By being able to tell his altitude, then you could always have the altitude advantage.

Captain Hawkins: If you had his altitude, well, the fighter director officer could put you in perfect position: 2,000 feet above him and behind him. The fallacy of the radar we had then was the fact that it had no altitude readout, and also it was only line of sight. If the Japanese planes came in low on the water, you just didn't pick them up. So they put the antennas as high on the ship as they could to take it out as far as possible. Those reserve

---

[*] CIC--combat information center.
[†] For a detailed memoir of one of these Naval Reserve fighter director officers, see John Monsarrat, Angel on the Yardarm: The Beginnings of Fleet Radar Defense and the Kamikaze Threat (Newport: Naval War College Press, 1985). Monsarrat served in the USS Langley (CVL-27), a sister ship of the two carriers from which Hawkins flew during the war.

officers came in and stuck with it. They lived with it from start to finish, and they did a fantastic job.

Q: Did the Japanese ever seem to be able to adjust to this and improve their tactics?

Captain Hawkins: They didn't seem to. For instance, I remember when we were in the Philippines. We started hitting the Philippines at Mindanao, the big island south. We hit that for three days. We'd pull off, replenish, move up to the next island, and hit that for three days. Pull out, go up, hit the next one. Every time we'd hit Mindanao, Los Negros, the middle island, and we moved up to Clark Field.* That was about the fourth set of raids. You'd think they'd be ready. They know you're coming. I went in on the fighter sweep, the first one to hit Clark Field. We went in there, dived in, dropped our bombs on the field, got close to the runway, and pulled back up. We were getting ready to hassle with whoever was around, and here it is, smoke and burning where all these bombs went off.

Then here came a big old Emily, which was their big flying boat.† It was approaching from out at sea and coming straight in at Clark Field. We were in there, just bombing the hell out of it, and here he came, straight in. So we took care of him, and then we got back up. We were circling over Clark Field, and here came a flight of 12 Topsys, which were similar to our old DC-3s.‡ They flew right across Clark Field and came right under where we were orbiting, just as if they had no communications--nothing. Those things didn't last very long at all; they were just gone. Finally, they evidently got some

---

* Clark Field was a U.S. Army Air Forces base on the island of Luzon, north of Manila. It had been captured by the Japanese at the outset of the war and served thereafter as their largest base outside the homeland. It was recaptured by U.S. forces under General of the Army Douglas MacArthur, USA, in January 1945.
† "Emily" was the Allied code name for the Japanese Navy's H8K Kawanishi patrol seaplane.
‡ "Topsy" was the Allied code name for the Mitsubishi Type 100 twin-engine transport plane.

fighters up from another field, and they came over and tangled with us over Clark. Still, with all this going on, a plane came in from way out.

You think, "Well, don't they have any communications? Don't they know that we've hit here three days, been gone a day, and come back, and now we're going to be here tomorrow or the next day, so they should be ready?" They didn't seem to. At least that particular time they certainly didn't, because I wouldn't have been within 40 miles of that thing if I knew they were in there bombing and raising cain. Now, if you're a fighter, that's something else; you come in and tangle with them. But not 12 Topsys coming right over the field or a big old P-boat to come back in over the field. That was just stupid. We never understood them.*

Q: Did you feel a hatred toward the Japanese at that point?

Captain Hawkins: Initially I had because of my brother's death. It was just a feeling that I had to get into it. I guess it was revenge, if you want to call it that. But when I shot down a guy, I just felt, "Well, I bested him. He would have gotten me, but I bested him." There was no hatred. We'd have reports of them shooting at some of our guys in parachutes and other things, you know, to build up a little hate and discontent. But we had only one case where a guy was strafed after he got in the water. Other than that, we had no reason to hate them, because they hadn't done anything other than to say, "I'm fighting for my side, and you're fighting for your side, so who can outdo the other one?"

Q: Did you get into any action with the kamikazes?

---

* This strike was on 13 September 1944, when Hawkins raised his total aircraft shot down to 14 by downing 1 Val dive-bomber and 3 Topsys.

Captain Hawkins: No. We had left the Cabot by the time the Belleau Wood was hit.* We picked up the Belleau Wood after she had gone to get repaired and then come back. We left the Cabot for three months, and that was the big kamikaze run. She took a hit, but we weren't there.†

Q: Where were you then?

Captain Hawkins: We were back in Hollister, California, reforming. The ship stayed out there, and we came off. We had been aboard for more than a year.‡ They took us off, put us on a ship, and brought us back to the States. We turned our airplanes over to Air Group 29. They just came aboard, moved in, and we came back.

Q: What was the rationale--just to give you a rest?

Captain Hawkins: Yes. We were the senior group out there. Everybody else had returned, but we hadn't. We had been there a long time. Oddly enough, the ship stayed, so it didn't help the crew very much.

Q: How did you spend that time in between?

---

* The USS Belleau Wood was hit by a Japanese kamikaze on 30 October 1944 while operating with Task Group 38.2 off Leyte. Following repairs at the San Francisco Navy Yard at Hunters Point, she rejoined the fleet at Ulithi Atoll on 29 January 1945.
† The Cabot was hit by a kamikaze on 25 November 1944, during air strikes against the island of Luzon in the Philippines. Her repairs were accomplished at Ulithi, and she rejoined the fleet in mid-December. At the time Air Group 29 was in the Cabot.
‡ Air Group 31 had joined the ship in the summer of 1943, when she began her shakedown cruise.

Arthur R. Hawkins #1 - 33

Captain Hawkins: Reforming. Well, we got new people. Some people got ordered out, and some of us stayed. We got a new CO of the squadron, and we just retrained in Hollister, California, getting the air group put back together again.*

Q: Probably got some good R&R too.†

Captain Hawkins: Oh, yes. Went to San Francisco and everything in that area. We managed to do our share of R&R. Of course, Hollister is a small town, you know. You had to go elsewhere if you went on liberty. It was just a field they had built up. Of course, they built fields all over the place in those times; they had to have them. Hollister was the one we drew.

Q: How much contact was there with the civilian populace during that time?

Captain Hawkins: Quite a bit, quite a bit. Usually you partied and everything as a group. It was just that type of a thing. Others would join in with you, and you'd pick up some civilians. I remember when we were getting ready to deploy the second time. Of course, rationing was on then. We were leaving San Francisco, and we were having a big party. Everybody had ended up with two or three bottles of champagne from somewhere. I don't know where we got them, but everybody had them. So we had them all iced down up in a room in the Fairmont.‡

---

* After being reformed it had few of the original pilots from Air Group 31. Commander Bruce S. Weber, USN, was the new air group commander and also commanding officer of the fighter squadron, VF-31, in which Hawkins served. Previously Lieutenant Commander Daniel J. Wallace, Jr., USN, was the commanding officer of VF-31 at Hollister but was killed on 5 March 1945 in a plane crash that took place during training.
† R&R--rest and recreation.
‡ The Fairmont is a large San Francisco hotel.

A civilian and his wife joined us. We had met them in the dining room or somewhere, told them we were having this party, and asked them to join us. They said, "Okay," and they joined us up in the room where the whole squadron was having this champagne just before we left. It turned out that this man was named Jantzen; he owned Jantzen swimsuits and so forth. We found this out when he went around and asked everybody what size trunks he wore. He was going to send us each a suit. Sure enough, out in the war zone, everybody ended up with a Jantzen swimsuit. I can't remember his or her first name, but I remember the incident in that area.

Q: It sounds as if aviators were pretty popular people at that point.

Captain Hawkins: Oh, yes. They were good guys. They were crazy guys; that's for sure.

Q: That is the general reputation that aviators have when they get ashore.

Captain Hawkins: That's true--very, very true. Some of the things they did you wouldn't believe.

Q: Well, tell me anyway.

Captain Hawkins: In fact, our group was the one that you've heard of when the freight train was coming down. We were flying out of Hollister, and you know that railroad runs right straight up and down through the middle of California. I was senior enough by then that I had my own division. The leader of the second section of my division was out with his wingman. In the F6F you had one landing light. When you flicked a switch, it came down out of the wing and pointed ahead. He came head to head with this train, and he lowered the light. That light looked like another train coming. Afterward they had us all standing at attention, trying to find out who did that.

Q: I'll bet the train engineer was a little unnerved.

Captain Hawkins: And, of course, with the Army Air Corps out on the West Coast, we'd always end up in dogfights with them, you know, everywhere we'd go. In fact, it was so bad that they had patrols that they flew just trying to catch guys getting into stuff they shouldn't. They'd have these planes flying up and down trying to find out who was flying under these bridges and who was doing this type of thing, you know.

Q: Was there sort of a feeling that since you had survived combat you were safe and couldn't succumb to any of this foolishness?

Captain Hawkins: I don't know what it was. I think it was just that you had to have something to give you a thrill. You didn't think about the consequences. All aviators are hard shells. When their times comes, it's coming. They're not going to let that bother them. It has to be that way. Otherwise, if you're not that way, you're not going to be a good aviator; let's put it that way. A machine is capable of stopping at any minute, so what the heck? Just count on it not stopping--that's all.

Q: Then you formed up again.

Captain Hawkins: We formed up and went back out on the Monterey. We went out to Hawaii, and then we moved off the Monterey. She had to go through some more training or something, so we went onto the Belleau Wood for the rest of our combat duty, which consisted then of Okinawa and the main islands. We were hitting the islands of Japan all the time, bombing all their fields out, strafing all their airplanes on the ground, and we stayed on there all the way through until the war was over.

The latter part of the war was pretty dry for fighter pilots. There was not much to shoot at. We became bombers, and during the big strike on Kure, I had one of the four hits with 1,000-pound bombs on the battleship Ise, which we sank in Kure Harbor.* Other than that, we were just working up and down the coasts of the main islands, mowing the ground and banging up as many of them as we could.

Q: The Ise was one of those hermaphrodites with the flight deck aft, wasn't she?

Captain Hawkins: Yes, she had a small deck back there. I don't know what they used it for.

Q: It sure was impractical as anything.

Captain Hawkins: She was a good battleship, but she was sitting on the mud by the time we had finished with her. And I was in the air on the last day of the war, after the bomb had been dropped at Hiroshima.† We were going in on a strike. I had a 1,000-pound bomb on board. The rest of the planes in my flight had bombs. We were going in with our target assignment, and we got a call that the war was over and the message, "Jettison your bombs in the water." So we did. We jettisoned our bombs, and the flight headed back in. The Japanese airplanes started showing up all over the place. They were getting in the air, heading out toward the fleet. So we reported that there were bogeys on the screen, and it looked like activity was picking up. Of course, we didn't know if it was sightseers coming out to see the fleet or if it was kamikazes coming out to get in their last match. So word came back from the admiral, "Shoot them down in friendly fashion."‡ That's what we did. There were about four or five airplanes shot down that day because they headed for the fleet and wouldn't turn away.

---

* This strike was on 28 July 1945.
† B-29 bombers of the U.S. Army Air Forces dropped atomic bombs on Hiroshima, Japan, on 6 August 1945 and on Nagasaki, Japan, on 9 August 1945. Hostilities ended shortly afterward, on 15 August.
‡ This statement is attributed to Admiral William F. Halsey, Jr., USN, Commander Third Fleet.

So then there was just drudgery from that until we went back home. There wasn't much of anything that missed me. It was all the happenings of the latter part of the war that were of any significance. New airplanes showed up; the Japs started out with what they called the Jack.[*] It was a very nice fighter. We only tangled with them one time. I didn't get to fire in anger at any of them, but I was on a flight that was jumped by four Jacks, and they shot down three of them. It was a really good-looking airplane--pointed nose. It was supposed to be much better than the Zero, but it was too late in the war. We never had to worry about them.

Q: Anything else to wrap up your war tour?

Captain Hawkins: No, that about does it. We stayed there and finished off in the main islands and were in the big fiasco during the signing on the Missouri.[†] They launched every airplane in the fleet to have them flying over the Missouri at the time. Man, you should have been there. It was something, I'll tell you. We had, let's see, 16 carriers. I guess the big ones had about 100 airplanes each, and the CVLs around 36. So probably more than 1,000 airplanes flew over. Then from Iwo Jima they sent in the B-29s.[‡] It turned out the weather wasn't too good. The ceiling was down to about 1,500 or 2,000 feet. Everybody was trying to get down under it so he could be seen over the Missouri. So here came the carrier flight of 1,000 or so airplanes going this way, and then there were about 50 or 60 B-29s coming the other way, under this low overcast. It was impressive. Nobody got killed. It had to impress them, because planes were going in all directions everywhere.

---

[*] "Jack" was the Allied code name for the Japanese J2M Mitsubishi land-based fighter.
[†] The battleship Missouri (BB-63) was the site of the Japanese signing of surrender documents in Tokyo Bay on 2 September 1945.
[‡] The B-29 Superfortress was a large four-engine Army Air Forces bomber. This was the same type of plane that dropped atomic bombs on Japan in August 1945.

Q: Did you get involved at all in picking up POWs?*

Captain Hawkins: Not picking them up. One of the stipulations was that they had to mark their camps after the Japanese surrendered. We would go in and search them out and take our torpedo bombers in to drop food, clothing, and whatever to them. But that was about the extent. We didn't actually bring them out and so forth.

Q: When did your ship go back home?

Captain Hawkins: We pulled in and anchored for a while in Tokyo Bay after the signing on the Missouri. Then some of us left and rode back to the West Coast because they had the point system then. If you had 58 points or 98 points, or whatever it was, you could be sent back and discharged.†

Q: Had it been your intent to be in for just the duration of the war?

Captain Hawkins: At that time, yes. No thought of going in or out then. We hadn't got all the way back to the States when I came off. They went around and said, "Okay, you, you and you have points. You're going back." And I was with a bunch that had points. I came off the Belleau Wood and went over to Eniwetok, where they said, ""We're sending you back to the States."‡

They had then started setting up how to get everybody back, and, of course, there were millions of people there. It looked like we were going to be there at Eniwetok for a long time before we got back. So four of us got together and found a boat. We went

---

* POWs--prisoners of war.
† For the demobilization of the U.S. armed forces after World War II, the services had a point system to determine individual priorities for leaving the service. Points were awarded for length of service, overseas service, battle stars, decorations, and dependent children. Those with the highest number of points were the earliest discharged.
‡ Eniwetolk is an atoll in the northwest Marshall Islands.

around to a lot of merchant ships sitting there and asked them if they had any room aboard. We found one ship that was going to Panama, and it had a hospital which they didn't use. They had six beds in the hospital and told us if we wanted to use that, fine.

We said, "Yeah, we'll take it." So we went back in, and they wouldn't give us orders. We had to boondoggle our orders out of some yeoman, and we got aboard this merchant ship. It took 31 days to go from Eniwetok to Balboa, Panama, on that eight-knot merchant ship. We got into Balboa, and the ship was quarantined. I went to see the skipper, and I said, "Send a dispatch in to the Navy that we're aboard." He got on the flashing light and sent it in that he had four naval officers on board for discharge.

Panic hit the button: "Where did they come from?" and all this. They came out in the admiral's barge and picked us up. They flew us on over to the other side of Panama and put us back into one of these units for shipping everybody home. Again, it looked like we were going to be there for four or five months, so we started hustling around to find a way back to the States. We were in the O-club having a beer when we ran into a PBM pilot who was down from Miami.* We found out he was going back to Miami the next day, so we asked him if he could take four. "Oh, yeah."

So we had to go boondoggle orders out of a yeoman again. We finally got them out of him and ended up in Miami. So they sent me to Corpus Christi and discharged me, whether I wanted to or not. I had applied for regular Navy at that time, but if I didn't make it, I didn't want to stay in the reserve. So I went on out and went back to college, going to the University of Cincinnati at that time. Then I got the word that I made USN.

Q: What month did you get discharged?

Captain Hawkins: That was October of '45. I was out about eight and a half months. Then I came back in and actually didn't get to flying until November of '46.

---

* O-club--officers' club; PBM was a Navy patrol seaplane.

Q: Did you get in one year of school at Cincinnati?

Captain Hawkins: Almost a year up there. And since I was working, I wasn't taking a full course. I was there for about eight months of school, then came back in. I reported in to Jacksonville, Florida, flying OS2Us and SCs.[*]

Q: Why did you make the switch from fighters to scout planes?

Captain Hawkins: I didn't make it; the Navy did. Actually, as you know, each battleship and cruiser had an aviation unit on board. You usually had four aviators on board ship--a senior aviator and three junior officers--and you had a crew of about 22 who maintained the airplanes. The battleships generally carried three planes, and the cruisers had two. After the war was over, they still had the brownshoe-blackshoe thing.[†] They didn't get along too well all along, I guess, and they just got fed up. All the senior aviators got out, because they'd had it, so it ended up they had no senior aviators. There might have been some junior ensigns and a few others still there, but no senior aviators. They were looking for lieutenants, so they took 14 fighter pilots and sent us through training to replace the senior aviators they had lost.

Q: That was quite a comedown.

---

[*] The Vought OS2U Kingfisher was the principal floatplane used by U.S. battleships and cruisers in World War II for rescue, scouting, and spotting the fall of shot. The Curtiss SC-1 Seahawk was a floatplane that entered fleet service in October 1944 as a replacement for the OS2U.

[†] Aviators often wore brown shoes with their khaki uniforms and green uniforms. They thus acquired the nickname "brownshoes" to distinguish them from the traditional surface ship officers, who were known as "blackshoes."

Captain Hawkins: In those days it didn't last long. I went to the Portsmouth, which was a light cruiser.* She was a flagship for ComNavMed.† I did two cruises on her, six months and six months.

Q: At what point did you switch from the OS2U to the SC-1?

Captain Hawkins: The OS2U just for training, and then we went in the SC-1. All the flying on board ship was done on SC-1s.

Q: Compared with the carriers, there was quite a difference in how you got back aboard ship.

Captain Hawkins: Well, the recovery was made with the ship turning into the wind and creating a slick inside the wind line. Then you came in and landed on the slick that they had created by making this sharp turn. The ship was dragging a sled made out of rope, and you taxied up until a hook on the bottom of the plane's float caught on this net. Once you were caught on that net, it just pulled you along until you hooked on.

Getting back aboard with the old OS2U wasn't too bad, because you had a crewman to do a lot of the work for you. He got out and hooked the plane onto the crane and so forth, while you were maintaining the airplane if it needed to be maintained. But with the SC, you were in a single-seater and had no crewman. So you had to make your own landing. You cut the engines and everything stopped. You had to hang a foot out of the cockpit, then reach around and get your sling. When the big crane came down, you hooked onto it, then jumped back in the cockpit. Then they'd hoist you aboard, set you on the catapult, secure you, and take you out of the plane. Well, it wasn't uncommon in

---

* The USS Portsmouth (CL-102) was commissioned 25 June 1945. She had a standard displacement of 10,000 tons, was 610 feet long, and 66 feet in the beam. Her top speed was 33 knots. She was armed with twelve 6-inch guns and twelve 5-inch guns.
† ComNavMed--Commander U.S. Naval Forces Mediterranean.

rough seas that the plane would shake off the sled and start sliding aft while you were trying to do all this. Then you had to hustle yourself back into the cockpit, restart the engine, taxi back up, and pick up the sled again. It wasn't too good an operation for one man, although it worked out all right.

Back in the stern we had a small hangar deck where we could put one airplane. So we had two catapults and one hangar. With the coming of the helicopter, it became obvious that the use for the scout and observation plane was fading. I convinced them to take one catapult off our ship. We didn't need two. We could put one plane in the hangar and one on the cat and launch two almost as fast as we could with two cats. So after they took off one catapult, it was easy to convince them to take the other cat off, and then you had a perfect deck for a helo. I'd say after my reign as senior aviator, there were very few more tours before the helo came aboard and became the observation plane, or scout, or whatever they needed for the battlewagons and cruisers.

Q: What were the SCs actually used for during that period?

Captain Hawkins: Well, you still were there for scouting purposes. You were a spotter for the main battery, and you could do search and rescue. Even though you were a single-seater, you could go out, land, and pick up somebody. In the back you had a cot; you could pull your seat forward and slide somebody back in there and bring him back. But with the radar improving so much and so forth, it was getting to the point where spotters were not necessary. Very few instances where you were needed in there to tell them to raise, lower, right, left, or whatever to get on target. The radar got such that they could do that better than a spotter could.

Q: Did you get some specialized training in spotting?

Captain Hawkins: Oh, yes.

Q: When was that?

Captain Hawkins: Well, you'd do it with your own ship, usually during the ORI or something like that, when they'd go down to the islands off Cuba.* And we had ranges off of Norfolk which they actually fired on. You would go in and spot for them, put them on target. Once they were on target, they'd fire for effect, and your job was done. They were on their own, and they didn't lose it after that.

Q: You talked about the camaraderie between the aviators and the ship's company in the Cabot. How was it when you were in the Portsmouth?

Captain Hawkins: Well, just that old brownshoe-blackshoe thing is always there. Being a fighter pilot, I got squared away in a hurry. I came aboard, and I couldn't get on my hangar deck because it had so much stuff on it. I found out it belonged to the gunnery department or the engineering department. They had a bunch of propellers back there and so forth. All the ships have a manual that they live by; this is the way the ship runs. One time they pulled something on me, and they said, "Here it is in the book. We can put stuff in your hangar deck for so and so. It's right there."

So I read the book. As the senior aviator, I was a department head, but I was not in the stateroom that the book said was supposed to be assigned. So I went to the skipper and said, "I'd like to have my stateroom."

"Yep, you read it." Well, the chaplain lived in my stateroom, so the chaplain had to move. In the book it said that his stateroom was supposed to be some other place. So then somebody else had to move. So they realized that the senior aviator on board was not going to take much of this bull. I got along great with them from then on.

---

* ORI--operational readiness inspection.

Q: That book was a two-edged sword.

Captain Hawkins: That's right. They were sorry they ever let me in on it.

I had three junior officers. I had a jaygee, two ensigns, 22 enlisted men, and two airplanes. We all stood deck watches, just like the rest of them. We all qualified as OOD under way, and we stood our turns.* As far as the skipper of the ship was concerned, my junior aviators were as good watch standers as any of them. Of course, they should be. They were up on relative motion, their navigation, and so forth. He told me one day he was as happy to have them on deck as any of the officers he had on board.

Q: Who was the skipper?

Captain Hawkins: His name was Maher.† The other day I looked through some of my orders, and I saw his name. He was a very good skipper, very good. He ran a good ship.

Q: For a career naval aviator, that was excellent shipboard training.

Captain Hawkins: It was. For me it couldn't have happened better, because I was able to get qualified as OOD under way and get all those tickets taken care of. Then, luckily enough, leaving that I went right back to the type of flying that I wanted to be doing.

Q: What about your Mediterranean cruises? What can you say about those?

Captain Hawkins: Well, being the flagship, we went to all the better ports. Our flying was mostly training, although we did a lot of pickups for the ship. Like we would fly down to Gibraltar and pick up mail, for instance. When the ship was in Naples, we'd put

---

* OOD--officer of the deck.
† Captain Arthur L. Maher, USN.

the plane over the side, go down, pick up mail, and come in on some ship and bring it back. The flying during those times, as you know, was a show effort. Basically what we did was show the flag. The training we did would sometimes be spotting training, practice with the gunnery department or practice to give the CIC people something to work with. And we'd run in those days--hardly ever ran with the carriers like they do nowadays.

The Little Rock was the other flagship that they swapped off back and forth on. We'd leave, and the flag would move over to the cruiser Little Rock. When we came back, they'd move it aboard us. So it was that type. Flying was just flying--no operational commitments other than to show the flag.

Q: How does one go from that to joining the very elite Blue Angels? Did you put in a request?

Captain Hawkins: No, I got my orders from the cruiser back to IATU, which is the instructors' training unit in Jacksonville.* It was the unit that trained instructors that went all over the training command.

Q: This was in the spring of 1948.

Captain Hawkins: Yes, that's when I joined IATU, and the Blues were attached to IATU. It just so happened they were having a couple of pilots turning over at that time, and they approached me to join the team. I guess it was because of my war record. In those days, it was a recruiting thing altogether. So they asked me, and, of course, I had the time. The team was flying F6Fs at that time, and they went into F8Fs right that same year. The F6F had just faded out.

We moved to Corpus Christi from Jacksonville right after that. The team operated out of Corpus with F8Fs. Then the jets came out, and they wanted us to go into jets, so

---

* IATU-intermediate air training unit.

we moved to Whiting Field down here.* Whiting Field was the only jet squadron training unit that the Navy had at that time. We actually didn't go through the training unit. We went to the West Coast and Air Group Five, VF-51. That was the only jet squadron in the operating fleet, so anybody who flew jets had to go out there to be checked out.

Q: What was the plane?

Captain Hawkins: They had the TOs, we called them, TV-2.† It was a Lockheed Shooting Star. And, of course, the Navy's Fury was the first jet that they had, the North American.‡ Air Group Five was the one that got them.

Q: So the TV was the training plane?

Captain Hawkins: Yes.

Q: And that prepared you for the FJ?

Captain Hawkins: Yes, that's the way they ran it out there. But we went out and got checked out in the trainer, the TO, and then came back and picked up our F9Fs. See,

---

* Whiting Field is at Milton, Florida, about 20 miles from Pensacola.
† In 1948 the Navy acquired a batch of Air Force F-80C Shooting Stars for use as jet advanced trainers. They were initially designated TO-1, later TV-1 after the Navy changed Lockheed's designation letter from O to T. In 1949 the Navy began procurement of a two-seat trainer developed for the Air Force. The designation of these planes was TO-2, later changed to TV-2.
‡ The FJ-1 Fury, built by North American Aviation, was the first jet fighter to go to sea operationally. The only squadron to get the FJ-1 model was VF-5A, later VF-51. The first carrier landings were on 10 March 1948. The FJ-1 was 34 feet long; wing span of 38 feet; gross weight of 15,600 pounds; and top speed of 547 miles per hour. It was armed with six .50-caliber machine guns.

that's what it amounted to. We picked them up at the plant, got checked out in the F9F at the Grumman plant, and flew them all in to Whiting Field.*

Q: How much was the change for you in going from a prop plane to a jet?

Captain Hawkins: An awful lot as far as the tight formation flying we were doing close in. You're so used to a lot of rudder pressure--fighting the rudder, fighting the torque, and so forth. Once you had the jets, you had no rudder to speak of. It was there, but it didn't do much for you. And the acceleration was gone. It was slow acceleration, whereas with the F8F you had instantaneous acceleration. You got out of position and could get back in in a hurry. So it was a lot of getting used to in the jet--lead and lag type of thing. You have to be able to anticipate when you're going to need a lot of power in a minute. You had to get going before you needed it, really, is what it amounted to.

Q: You had to plan a little more.

Captain Hawkins: That's right. Then you didn't worry about a prop and whether it was going to cut somebody's tail off. All in all, it certainly turned out an easier airplane to fly formation in, although it wasn't as spectacular, because you couldn't do the things that you could do in the F8F. That Bearcat could do a show and stay right in front of the crowd and never leave the confines of the field. With the jet you had to take it out and turn it around and give it a little leeway; that spread the show out. With the F8F you could do stuff like a loop on takeoff, whereas you were certainly not going to do that with a jet--not

---

* The Grumman F9F-2 Panther was first delivered to an operational unit, Fighter Squadron 51, in May 1949. On 3 July 1950 the Panther became the first U.S. Navy jet ever used in combat. The F9F-5 model was 39 feet long; wing span of 38 feet; gross weight of 18,721 pounds; and top speed of 579 miles per hour. It was armed with four 20-millimeter guns.

those we had then, anyway. You still can't do it now, but you can at least climb out and do a Cuban 8 or something on takeoff.*

Q: How did you learn the routines and so forth for the air shows?

Captain Hawkins: Well, you'd start out with two of you flying wing. I mean, you'd go out and just fly wing on one guy and do rolls, loops, nip-ups--nothing you hadn't done all your life in an airplane anyway in tail chasing and stuff. It's just a matter of, "Okay, we're going to formalize this thing and do something where each guy knows what he's doing." Then the four of you would go out with a leader and just practice. That's all it amounted to.

Of course, the routine would be changed as you went along. We were shooting for about a 30-minute routine, so we'd put in new maneuvers or take maneuvers out. We'd try out new things to see how well they worked. Once you got the routine down, it was a set routine for that show. You knew what was coming next and so forth. You'd have to vary it only if something happened during the show. If some airplane flew across the field, for example, then you had to change the routine. Otherwise, you knew what was coming next, expected it, knew what the routine was going to be. All that was required then was for the leader just to say one word, and you were into the next maneuver.

Q: Did you ever have any problem where some guy went the wrong way or forgot the assignment?

Captain Hawkins: Well, in trying to establish new maneuvers sometimes you might go astray a little. With the F8Fs we wanted to try a snap roll in place. We never did anything

---

* The Cuban 8 is a maneuver in which the pilot pulls up in a loop. When coming down the backside of the loop, he rolls level and continues straight ahead. By then, while going the opposite direction from which he started, he pulls up in another loop and again rolls level on the back side of the loop and exits straight ahead. Viewed from the side, the maneuver looks essentially like a figure 8.

where you were blind at any point in a maneuver. Supposedly, that's what we tried to do. However, we figured with a snap roll you'd be over so fast you wouldn't let it bother you. So we had three of them trying it. I wasn't in this flight, but there were three of them going to do it in a V before they put a man in the slot to do it. And on signal they snapped. The right wingman ended up over on the wing of the left wingman, so we scrapped that. That didn't work. We went back to not doing any maneuver where you're blind at any time. They do some maneuvers nowadays where they are somewhat blind, but they're not tight formation maneuvers, so they can get away with them.

Q: What was the feeling about being in an outfit that was not in the mainstream. Obviously, it was not an operational squadron. Was that a plus or a minus as far as your career was concerned?

Captain Hawkins: Well, actually, career-wise it hurts and helps. Certainly, it's like losing two years from an active-duty outfit, doing the gunnery, bombing, and other things that you would be doing. However, once you leave, the prestige of having been in it is certainly a plus. As far as it goes now, the Blue Angels do shows 52 weeks a year. You can imagine going on the road and living out of suitcases. It's not the glamour that it's cracked up to be, really, but it's certainly enjoyable flying.

Q: You get the kind of applause and public recognition that is afforded to very few in the Navy in that way.

Captain Hawkins: That's true, but you try to hold it down as much as you can, because there aren't many naval aviators that couldn't do the same thing if they were pulled in as trainees to fill openings. The Blue Angels now have qualifications that you have to meet--so many hours in a jet and so forth---before you can even apply. There are other things that you have to take into consideration--living close together and public relations. But it's still sort of a personal selection.

The members on the team are those that volunteer. When someone reports aboard now, the whole team gets to meet and greet him and find out about him before they say, "Well, I think you can hack it." Flight-wise you don't know until you get him in the air, but if he's gotten that far you know that he's got the capability of doing it. But some people just can't live in a group like that. You certainly don't want a man who's got a drinking problem or any kind of problem that would reflect back on the Navy. It's a close-knit unit. Since '46 there have not been even 200 pilots in it.

Q: It's a real honor.

Captain Hawkins: It's a small group. They are a squadron now, by the way.

Q: Oh, I didn't know that.

Captain Hawkins: Yes, they're an official squadron, although they don't train in gunnery and so forth like that.

When the Korean War started, we had been flying jets, and they needed a jet squadron. We had men trained and everything else. So that became the nucleus of VF-191, which was already a squadron, but they weren't flying jets. We took all our expertise and all our men, plunked them in a squadron, and did our own checking out of the pilots and crew. They didn't have the RAG squadrons and things like the ones now that do all that.[*]

Q: This was in July 1950 that you got switched over.

Captain Hawkins: Yes.

---

[*] A replacement air group (RAG) squadron provides training in a particular aircraft for pilots going to operational squadrons that use that plane.

Q: What was your job within the squadron?

Captain Hawkins: I was operations officer. It ended up that each one of the Blues had his own division. So he picked up three kids and formed a four-man unit. It worked out well that way.

Q: The Navy had gone way down by that point, so it needed a quick transfusion.

Captain Hawkins: Sure. The ship we went aboard came out of mothballs, and we went right aboard. She came down there from Bremerton.[*]

Q: Which one was that?

Captain Hawkins: Princeton.[†] We went aboard, carqualed, and shoved off.

Q: You had enough experience that I would think the qualification process could be compressed.

Captain Hawkins: Yes. And all the pilots we picked up had been flying the F8F in the squadron. It was just a matter of switching them over to jets. The routine techniques and so forth are certainly not that much different as far as combat tactics are concerned, whether it's jet or prop. So, really, we took our airplanes and plugged them into the

---

[*] Many of the ships put into the Pacific Reserve Fleet after World War II were berthed at the Puget Sound Naval Shipyard, Bremerton, Washington.
[†] The USS Princeton (CV-37) was commissioned 18 November 1945. She had a standard displacement of 33,300 tons, was 888 feet long, 93 feet in the beam, an extreme width of 148 feet on the flight deck, and had a draft of 29 feet. She had a top speed of 33.5 knots and could accommodate approximately 90 aircraft.

squadron, and we started checking them out with those as new planes came in. We finally ended up with 24 birds. We had our squadron formed and then went on to Korea.

Q: That was the second time you had gone to war in a carrier that was just commissioned.

Captain Hawkins: Commissioned the second time. The Princeton had gone into mothballs and come out again.*

Q: How soon did you get over to Korea?

Captain Hawkins: I'll have to look at my log book again. August of '50 we started in the squadron. October of '50 we were in Korea.

Q: What kind of missions were you flying there?

Captain Hawkins: They were mostly recon missions.† We were doing regular fighter combat air patrol, but mostly it was recon. We would go in, and they had the routes all laid out that we would interdict every day. We would be assigned a Purple One or Purple Three, which was a certain route that went all the way up. We'd keep that route clean all day by flying up and down it.

Then we started putting bombs on the airplane, which was the first time the jets had ever had bombs on board. So we decided to try it. We had been carrying rockets, because the bomb racks were equipped for that. So we started out with 250-pounders

---

* The Princeton had been decommissioned on 29 June 1949 and was recommissioned on 28 August 1950.
† Recon--reconnaissance.

inside and with 100-pounders all the way out. We did the first carrier launch with bombs.[*] In fact, I did the first flight. We went in, and they were time-delay fuzes for a low-altitude drop. We knocked out a bridge just on the initial hop. So that was the start of it. From then on, we always carried bombs when we went on a flight, even doing interdiction. We'd carry bombs, rockets, or the armor-piercing rockets for tanks and so forth.

Our big problem was operating jets when the carriers hadn't operated them before very much. It was getting used to the short legs. Instead of a four-hour turnaround, it had to be a two-hour turnaround. Once that got going, we cycled the jets every two hours. We'd go in low and drop our bombs, but we couldn't stay in there and wait for a call. We'd go in and have the target sighted by the time we got there if we were on a call mission. On a recon you had to be at low altitude to see the trucks or tanks or whatever was on the road.

We also had ADs on board and F4Us too.[†] They were on four-hour cycles, and we had to plug in between, which was pretty hard on a straight deck.[‡]

Q: Did you tangle with any MiGs over there?[§]

Captain Hawkins: Not at all. The areas were split up: the Navy's area and the Air Force's area. The Air Force area, naturally, was the northern area where all the MiGs came across. We did escort B-36s and B-29s, whatever would come in. Lots of times we would pick them up and act as escorts on the way in on their bombing runs and this type

---

[*] On 1 April 1951, Lieutenant Hawkins and Lieutenant Commander George B. Riley, USN, commanding officer of VF-191, scored four direct hits on the Songjin bridge in North Korea, using 250-pound bombs. It was the first bombing attack of the Korean War by naval jets. See Malcolm W. Cagle and Frank A. Manson, The Sea War in Korea (Annapolis: U.S. Naval Institute, 1957), page 238.
[†] The AD Skyraider and F4U Corsair were propeller-driven aircraft.
[‡] During the 1950s many of the Essex-class aircraft carriers were converted to angled flight decks that permitted simultaneous launching and recovery of aircraft. The Princeton was not converted and still had the axial deck she was built with.
[§] MiGs were Soviet-built jet fighters.

of thing. We did that several times, and the Air Force stopped that. They didn't want the Navy escorting their airplanes, so they started escorting them.

Q: The Air Force planes would have a ways to fly from Japan to get into position.

Captain Hawkins: Yes, it was much better for us to do it, because we could pick them up right overhead. And we did it quite frequently, but we stopped doing it later when they wanted to do it.

Q: Interservice jealousy.

Captain Hawkins: That's what it was, for sure.

Q: I've seen a picture from the Princeton from that era, and somebody had made a remark that they dropped everything but the kitchen sink. So then they put a kitchen sink on the bottom of one of the Princeton's planes and dropped it on Korea.[*]

Captain Hawkins: Well, that's true. We were the ones also that dropped torpedoes against the dams, if you've seen pictures of that. It was our air group that did that, trying to knock out the dams with torpedoes, which worked. They were the only torpedoes dropped in anger since World War II.

Q: Who was your air group commander?

Captain Hawkins: Well, our skipper was Johnny Magda, who had been the skipper of the

---

[*] For more details see the Naval Institute oral history of Vice Admiral Paul D. Stroop, USN (Ret.), who commanded the Princeton in 1951-52.

Blues and then took over VF-191.* The air group commander's name was Merrick.†
Now, Johnny was killed, and so was Merrick. Johnny was killed on a flight over Wonsan,
during the landings and so forth over there when we were having trouble getting the
Marines back down out of the Chosin Reservoir.‡

Q: Your problems then were primarily operational-type accidents?

Captain Hawkins: Yes. We got a lot of flak from low-altitude work, but there was no
worry of air-to-air combat. It was just drudgery every day of doing the same thing over
and over. When you got hit, it was usually from rocket fire--low-caliber stuff, low
altitude. Other than that, there weren't any missiles or anything to worry about. You
worried about bombing yourself on this low-altitude stuff.

Q: Did you get any R&R breaks during that period?

Captain Hawkins: Well, we'd come back to some little island and drink some beer or
something. But we stayed until our tour was up.

Q: Did you get into medicinal alcohol aboard ship?

Captain Hawkins: Oh, yes. You got your brandy every so often. And our skipper would
break out the beer every so often after a replenishment. Every man got two cans of beer.
Of course, there were always those that didn't drink, so somebody else ended up with
theirs.

---

* Lieutenant Commander John J. Magda, USN, commanding officer of Fighter Squadron 191.
† Commander Richard C. Merrick, USN Commander Carrier Air Group 19 until he was shot down and killed on a close air support mission on 29 May 1951.
‡ Magda was killed in March 1951.

Q: The skipper wasn't too popular with the ship's company at that point, was he?

Captain Hawkins: Well, this wasn't just for the aviators. He'd break out beer for everybody after a big replenishment or something.

Q: Who was that skipper?

Captain Hawkins: The ship skipper was one of the famous brothers Gallery. Dan was the admiral, and Bill was the CO of the Princeton.[*]

Q: What do you remember about Bill Gallery?

Captain Hawkins: Couldn't ask for a better skipper. He just died recently.[†] We have a big golf tournament and banquet every year, and he was just here for it. Right after that he died.

He was such a peach of a guy that when it came time for him to leave the ship, the crew started getting money together to buy him a present. He came on the 1MC and said, "Look, I know this is going on, and you can't do it. I can't accept a gift. It's against the regs."[‡] So he was going to stop us from raising money. But the crew raised enough money to buy his wife a Cadillac and presented it to her on the dock when he got in.

---

[*] Rear Admiral Daniel V. Gallery, Jr., USN, was known for his June 1944 capture of the German submarine U-505. He later wrote a number of popular books about the Navy. His oral history is in the Naval Institute collection. Captain William O. Gallery, USN, commanded the Princeton from her recommissioning on 28 August 1950 until relieved on 11 August 1951.

[†] Gallery, who retired in 1955 as a rear admiral, died on 15 November 1981.

[‡] The 1MC is a ship's general announcing system. There are loudspeakers in various compartments throughout a ship.

Q: He must have been popular.

Captain Hawkins: He was. He was a great guy. He was a CO that everybody loved. They'd have done anything for him.

Interview Number 2 with Captain Arthur R. Hawkins, U.S. Navy (Retired)

Place: Naval Aviation Museum, Pensacola, Florida

Date: Friday, 15 July 1983

Interviewer: Paul Stillwell

Q: Captain, when we broke off yesterday, you were talking about your experiences serving in the carrier USS Princeton, which had been reactivated from mothballs for the Korean War.

Captain Hawkins: We recalled several reserve squadrons during the Korean War and formed the air groups and sent them out to combat zone. When other carriers showed up out there for the first time, we would go over to them. We would take about six or seven of our people and go over and help check them out for things we had learned from having the jets on board. We gave them suggestions on how to operate with them and also try to bring the reserve units up to snuff, so to speak, since they had been out of the mainstream for quite some time, other than being up on their flying and that part of the action. They needed a little guidance and bringing them up on the latest developments going on, and what they could accomplish.

Then Korea just sort of died out on us, as you know. It came and went.

Q: How long did it take the reservists to get acclimated to that routine?

Captain Hawkins: Well, they came out very fast. They recalled them and equipped them with new airplanes in most cases. Some of them had good airplanes, such as the ADs that they brought out. But all the jet squadrons that they had formed with these reserve pilots were fairly new. I'd say from four to five months from the time they recalled them they were on board ship and out in the war zone. So it was a credit to the reserve squadrons that they could do it. It was something that proved that the reserve units were something that you needed as backup, a pool to pull from when you needed them in a hurry. It was an area that they hadn't used them before, but it had been a viable program from essentially World War II.

Q: Was there any attempt to use the jets for close air support?

Captain Hawkins: Oh, yes. You had to develop your call missions before you left the ship. You would leave the ship with your target assigned, go in, hit your target, and return to ship. You talked to the air controller once you got in there, whenever you changed your hop. But the jets couldn't go in a circle and stay on station for any length of time at that low altitude. You'd get a call mission from the beach, "Strike coordinates B1-H7," or whatever the coordinates were, and report to ground controller such-and-such on channel so-and-so and arrive at a target. So you'd have your target assignment before you left the ship. In you'd go and report in to the ground controller, and if that was still your target, you hit it. If it wasn't, you changed it.

Most of the ground support, naturally, was done by the prop planes, which could stay on station for four or five hours with belly tanks and hit different targets on call. But the jets couldn't stay as long, and that's why they were used for interdiction most of the time. We'd have a route assigned, for instance, a highway that ran the full length of Korea, jump on it on one end, go all the way to the other end, turn around and come back, interdict the route to keep the traffic off of it. We'd report the movement of troops if we saw them, even though we couldn't do anything about them. We also tore up the railroad traffic and what have you, although there was a lot of State Department input to that Korean War. There were lots of things we couldn't hit that we would have liked to hit, but they were off-limits.

Q: I understand it was very difficult in some cases up near the Yalu River because of the restrictions. You could hit one end of a bridge, for example.*

Captain Hawkins: Yes. You could not go across. You could look across to see the place where the planes were taking off, but you couldn't go bomb it. So you'd sit on that side and wait for them to come over. Like you say, one end of the Yalu bridge you could bomb, and the other end was off-limits. And power plants and things like that were off-limits. I think they thought we would finish off the war in a hurry, and we didn't want to rebuild all that stuff. So it was pretty touch-and-go. A pilot in there just couldn't drop indiscriminately on whatever good target he saw. He was to hit tanks that day or trains that day or whatever he was to do. He was never assigned an indiscriminate target. Everything was assigned by the ground controllers or from the ship.

Q: Who were the ground controllers?

Captain Hawkins: You had a joint center which was run by the Air Force, a large center. All the target requests were fed through that. That was manned by Air Force, Navy, Army, and Marine. The calls would come in to this center for strike missions, say, and we'd strike over here, here, here, and here. They would coordinate through that center, and they would pass you off. Say it was a Marine request for bombing a certain grid position. You would receive your request for a mission from the center on the ground in Korea. Then you'd report in to them, and they would pass you off to the ground controller, who was right up front where the troops were. Maybe he would mark the target for you with an artillery shell or that type of thing, a smoke shell. There were several ways to mark a target. The Army and Marines had the little bitty cover airplanes

---

* The Yalu River separates North Korea from Communist China. The rules of engagement prevented offensive action across the Yalu, because President Harry S. Truman did not want to risk setting off a still wider war.

and SNJs too.* They could fire the smoke rockets that marked targets with that, and those gave the pilots a good pinpoint of what they were trying to hit.

Q: Did you get involved in coordinating your strikes with the gunfire ships, the battleships and cruisers?

Captain Hawkins: Oh, yes. As you know, during the Korean War they brought up some battleships again to reach back in. I mean, they had a 20-mile range with those guns of theirs. A lot of times we cleared the area, because you never knew the trajectory of what they were firing. They might be firing up high and the projectiles would fall over a mountain or that type of thing. We were well aware of when the gunfire was coming from the ships and to stay out of the area.

Q: Was that arranged through the ground controller also?

Captain Hawkins: Usually, yes. It was all brought through the center on requests. They then would give them their grid or targets and wherever they were and let them go.

Q: Those battleships had sort of a split personality in Korea, as they did during the World War II. They were both steaming with the fast carriers for AA protection and providing shore bombardment.†

Captain Hawkins: That's true, but in Korea you didn't worry about AA too much. We had supremacy in the air everywhere over Korea other than up in the outer corner where the all action and dogfights would go on every so often. But there was no air action down

---

* The SNJ Texan, a propeller plane built by North American Aviation, first went into service in the late 1930s as a trainer.
† AA--antiaircraft.

in Korea itself. We just never saw it. The fighting was nearly all on the ground, hiding in the bushes.

Q: Did you have any desire to get up into that dogfighting area?

Captain Hawkins: Oh, yes. We always wanted to, but you didn't cross that line. You stayed in your area. We always wanted to get a piece of the air action, but no way.

Q: How was the weather to operate in?

Captain Hawkins: Actually, it was just like flying over Iceland. During the time of the year when I was there it was just completely covered with white snow all over the place, all the mountain peaks and so forth. And from that you get fog and that type of thing. But, all in all, the weather was fairly good. You'd run into foggy mornings and that type of thing, but I don't recall many missions canceled because of weather. It was basically dry weather, so it was just cold. We'd get snow on the deck of the carrier. They found a good use for the jets; they'd turn up the jets and burn the snow off the deck. They finally decided there were other ways to do it better than that. By the time they turned the jets up and launched them usually the snow up front was all melted off the carrier, so they were in good shape.

Q: Did you ever have to land or take off in a snowstorm?

Captain Hawkins: No. I've been caught in fog a lot but never a snowstorm. Fog over in that area comes quickly. It'll be nice and clear, and ten minutes later it'll just change to zero-zero. So we had that. But usually it's a shallow fog; it's not over a couple of hundred feet deep. You can find your ships and manage to get back aboard. But with your fuel problems in the jets during that time, you got back aboard. You didn't have enough fuel for many passes to get onto the ship. When you came back, the ship turned into the wind and picked you up. It wasn't unusual at all for us to get back aboard with 200 or 300 pounds of fuel. Now, the safety factor is coming back aboard ship with 1,200 pounds. That would give us at least four or five passes around the ship. When we'd come back with 200 or 300 pounds, you got just one pass to get aboard. So on a straight-decker, it was a little hairy at times. But we never had any problems not getting aboard or having to go the beach or something. It just didn't happen.

Q: You mentioned yesterday that there had to be adjustments made in the carrier deck operations to accommodate the shorter cycle times of the jets.

Captain Hawkins: Yes.

Q: Were you also adjusting tactics and doctrine in the air because of the new planes and the different type of war?

Captain Hawkins: Well, no, that had nothing to do with the operation of the deck itself. When you change your tactics in airplanes as far as dogfighting or that type of thing, it's pretty much done before you come aboard. That's done with your carrier air group training back on the beach, wherever you may be. But the carrier's normal cycle was four hours. You'd send a flight off, and four hours later you'd send another one off and take that one back aboard. So if it was a half-deck launch, then the deck was always clean. You had one gone and you'd launch another one, the deck's clean and you could take the other group back.

But when the jets arrived on the scene, the cycle had to be shortened. During that time it was two hours, but now it's up to two and a half, three, four hours for the jets. I mean, it's according to what kind of mission you're on. In our case in Korea it was two hours because you'd go down low all the time. So you had to have a launch and then a jet recovery two hours later, and two hours later another launch. With a straight deck, that was quite a problem to work out. With the angled decks now it's not such a problem. You've got the deck clear back there to take them aboard while you can still be operating up front. On a straight deck you couldn't do that. You were coming into the pack all the time.

Q: That's where the air boss earns his pay.[*]

Captain Hawkins: Yes, he's a busy young fellow during those launches, landings, and the planning of the whole thing.

Q: Did that deployment come to an end while you were still in the squadron? Did you rotate back to stateside?

Captain Hawkins: Yes. The whole squadron came back to Moffett Field, which was our home field for the VF-191.[†] Then the squadron and air group started reforming. They pulled two of us that had been on the Blue Angels before and sent us back to Corpus Christi to help reform the Blue Angels. They had just determined that they wanted them back as a recruiting crew again. So they took myself and Pat Murphy.[‡]

Q: This was in late 1951?

Captain Hawkins: Yes. Pat Murphy and I both had been with the team before, when we formed the squadron, and we went back to Corpus Christi to help reform a team. We

---

[*] The air officer in an aircraft carrier's crew controls the operations of the flight deck and hangar deck.
[†] Moffett Field is in Sunnyvale, California. It was later decommissioned as part of the base-closure actions of the 1990s.
[‡] Lieutenant Francis J. Murphy, USN.

picked up new pilots, and as a matter of fact three of them came from VF-191. That way you knew who you were getting and knew their capabilities and so forth. Lieutenant Commander Butch Voris, who had formed the team originally back in Jacksonville in 1946, came down to Corpus Christi and helped reform the team and led it for almost a year.* Then in 1952 I took over from him as commanding officer of the Blues.

We were then flying the F9F-5s. We had flown the F9F-2s when we went into combat in VF-191, and the F9F-5, which is the next step in the series, had a little better engine and some other improvements. We flew the F9F-5s on up through '53. At the end of '53 we were assigned the F9F-6, which was our first swept-wing fighter.

Q: How did they compare in performance to what you had had before?

Captain Hawkins: The new ones were Mach 1. They were faster than the speed of sound, and they were just much more advanced aircraft. They had all the electrical trim tabs on the stick. They had the flying tail, the first one we ever had. And, of course, the engine was a little more powerful.

Q: What do you mean by flying tail?

Captain Hawkins: Well, on a normal aircraft, the elevator is part of the stabilizer. When you pull back the stick, it'll go up and down. When you go to a flying tail, if you rigidly lock that elevator to the stabilizer and free the stabilizer, then the whole stabilizer moves. It's done hydraulically. Instead of just the small elevator you're working with, you're working with the whole stabilizer. It was the first flying-tail aircraft that the Navy had, and it was hydraulically operated, which is like power steering. You pull back on the stick and the hydraulic system makes the whole stabilizer move. But you could freeze it and adjust to the regular elevator for low altitudes. All that did was give you a bigger bite at

---

* Lieutenant Commander Roy M. Voris, USN.

high altitudes, which let you turn tighter. And, because of the skinny air up there, it just gave you more control of the airplane. It was well designed but not too well thought out.

When we picked up the new aircraft for the Blues, we got six of the first 13 that the factory built.[*] We went up and checked out in them, then started home with them. I didn't make it home.[†] I had a little problem at about 42,000 feet as we climbed out on our way back to Corpus Christi. The flying tail ran away on me, and we found out later what happened. It was hydraulically operated, and it had a slip valve. When you pulled the stick back, it opened a little hole. The pressure went in and slid this valve back and forth, which made the stabilator go up and down.

Well, I developed a leak on the downside of this valve as we were going along, so it started nosing the airplane a little. It just nosed it on over and over and over, and it was going into an outside loop at 42,000 feet. At the bottom of this outside loop, which was at about 32,000 feet, I started redding-out, which is the opposite of blackout. You know, with negative G's your blood goes to your head, while in blacking out the blood is being pulled away from your head with positive G's. So I had to bail out of the thing.

It also had a new feature of being able to eject yourself through the canopy, which had never been done before, but which we had pioneered after Johnny Magda's death in Korea. We needed some way to get out of the airplane when you couldn't get rid of the canopy, because the normal procedure for ejecting from an airplane was first to blow the canopy off and arm your seat. This was done with one handle below in the cockpit. Then you had to pull the face curtain over your face to eject yourself out of the airplane. Well, Johnny Magda was killed in Korea, and we were almost sure that he couldn't eject his canopy. If you couldn't get the canopy off, you couldn't arm your seat. He went in and hit the water still in the cockpit and then was thrown out of the airplane.

So this F9F-6 had that feature built in. You could arm your seat with the canopy still on by an emergency arming device up next to your head. So in this situation of

---

[*] The Blue Angels picked up their new planes at the Grumman plant at Bethpage, Long Island, New York.
[†] This incident occurred on 4 August 1953.

negative G's that I was in, this outside loop that was being forced upon me by the flying tail going out of whack, I tried everything to get it out, but it just kept going under.

So with all those negative G's, I was pulled almost up into the canopy, and the arming device for arming and blowing the canopy was down on the left side. So there was only one thing to do: go through the canopy. It had never been done before, but somebody had to do it first, I guess. So I armed the seat and blew myself, seat and all, right through the Plexiglas of the canopy. Doing it that way probably saved my life, because the plane was already through the speed of sound. If I'd have blown the canopy, the slipstream would have just whipped me to death.

We knew of the case of an F-86 where a pilot had bailed out above the speed of sound, and he didn't live through it.[*] When they recovered his body, his face was just torn up where the wind had pulled his mouth open and all kinds of weird things. But in my case, going through the canopy, I had started slowing down immediately as soon as I had left the airplane. I was on the slow-down, not having to sit there in the seat with a canopy gone and this Mach 1 slipstream coming through. Although when I hit the slipstream, it tore off my oxygen mask and everything.

Here I was up at 32,000 feet with no oxygen and wanting to free-fall, because that was the only way to get down quickly to an altitude where I could breathe. I saw I was going to pass out, and I wasn't going to hit the ground passed out, so I deployed the chute anyway. So I was hanging in the chute while passed out. Now, we had been taught grunt breathing during training. There's oxygen at 30,000; it's just that the pressure's not there to force it into your lungs. So the basic pretext is to suck in a big breath and force pressure on your lungs to try to force some in your bloodstream, which I started doing. And it worked. I'd grunt-breathe and then force real hard and then be in the gray area, about to pass out again. Then I'd clear up as that blood with oxygen in it hit my heart. I did that grunt-breathing down to 15,000, until the area where oxygen was plentiful enough

---

[*] F-86 was the designation for the Air Force version of the Navy-developed FJ Fury.

to breathe. It took about 22 minutes from the time my chute deployed until I hit the ground, so I was there for a while.

Q: You were keeping time of all this?

Captain Hawkins: No. There were six of us together, and I was leading the six back to Corpus Christi. The others saw me pitch out of the formation and start down. Two of them started following me down. They never did see me bail out. They stayed with the airplane, because I bailed out upside down. I was hanging in the bottom. They followed the plane all the way down till it hit the ground and exploded. They started climbing back up and then they saw me coming down in the chute. They came up and started circling me, and I was at 22,000 then. So, all in all, they were the ones that did the timing--not me. I was too busy doing other things.

I came on down in the chute, and I hit in a cotton patch just outside of Pickens, Mississippi. There was a little town up there. In fact I was just driving through the other day past Pickens, Mississippi. I remembered my ordeal. Anyway, a farmer was in the local area and saw me coming down. People on the ground had heard the claps from the airplane passing through the sound barrier up there, and they looked up. There wasn't a thunder-bumper around anywhere, and then all of a sudden they saw this plane screaming down. They saw it hit and crash--luckily enough in a wooded area where it didn't bother anybody. So they came over to pick me up, and the planes were buzzing me back and forth to see if I was all right. I finally gave them a "Roger" signal to shove off. I assumed I was okay; I was alive. Three of them went into Memphis and landed there. Two of them went on into Barksdale in Shreveport.[*] They had stayed up and passed out messages to Barksdale to let them know what was going on, to tell them we had lost an airplane.

So the highway patrol came and picked me up in Pickens and took me to Jackson, Mississippi, where a Navy plane came to pick me up and flew me into Memphis. There

---

[*] Barksdale Air Force Base, Shreveport, Louisiana.

they took me to the hospital, looked me over, decided I was all right, and turned me loose. I stayed in Memphis that night and got to Corpus the next day. I had a few bruised ribs and frost-bitten ears, but other than that I was in great shape. I flew a show six days later, so I guess I was in much better shape than I should have been.

Q: It says something for Navy training that you had the presence of mind to do all the things you had to do.

Captain Hawkins: That's what your training is supposed to do, so it's done automatically. Without the training you wouldn't make it. You've got to do the training, have it instilled in you, and when the time comes you follow that procedure and then away you go.

At that time we did not have the modern-day things like chutes that would deploy themselves and oxygen bottles and that type of thing for bailing out. You free-fall and don't worry about it, because you have a barometer on your seat which is at a preset level, say, 5,000 feet, which pops and opens the chute for you; you don't have to do it yourself. During that time--that was '53--those things were there, but they hadn't started putting them in the aircraft yet. Now they have a chute that you can deploy the seat chute and everything off the catapult. It's a Martin Baker seat, which is a rocket-type seat that when you eject, the rocket shoots you up high enough for the chute to deploy. Everything is done automatically. You just have to do the ejecting. When you decide to go, you go, and then you depend on the automatic devices to take care of the rest of it to deploy and things like that.

So that was my only bail-out during my 31 years of flying.

Q: The Navy then had another new jet fighter that McDonnell put in, the Banshee.[*] Did you ever fly that to compare it with the Grumman planes you were flying?

---

[*] The McDonnell F2H Banshee entered the fleet in 1949. It was used during the Korean War and for several years thereafter.

Captain Hawkins: No, I never flew the Banshee. I was a Grumman man, I guess is what you'd say. I flew Grumman aircraft all my career until I got in an A4D squadron.[*] Of course, in my VX squadron there were all types of aircraft, including the F7U, which stayed with us a while.[†] It was a far advanced bird, but it just never did pan out. It was the first no-tail airplane, more or less designed on the old delta wing. Some people called it the Cadillac of the airplanes. It was a nice cross-country airplane.

I did the complete weapons test in VX-5, took it all the way through special weapons, designed the maneuvers for lofting and delivering the bomb and so forth.[‡] Then as CAG I flew all the airplanes in the air group.[§] Mostly I stuck with the Grumman aircraft, but the Douglas got the A4D out and Chance Vought, the F8U.[**] So those I flew up quite often.

Q: Was the experience during your second tour with the Blue Angels pretty much similar to the first as far as routines and so forth?

Captain Hawkins: Yes. You are always adding routines as you go along. You'll come up with a new maneuver and put it into the program. Basically it's the same right now as it was then. I mean, they do different things, but basically the maneuvers are still done in a diamond formation and echelon formation. The group now has added a delta formation which involves all six planes. They do only a couple of maneuvers with all six in formation. Little variations as you go along. Sometimes it will depend on the type of airplane you're flying, if you can put a maneuver in or not or keep doing a maneuver that they used to do. That type of thing.

---

[*] The McDonnell Douglas A4D Skyhawk was a light attack aircraft with a long history.
[†] The Vought F7U Cutlass went into service in 1952.
[‡] VX-5--Experimental Squadron Five.
[§] CAG--commander of a carrier air group.
[**] The Vought F8U Crusader entered the fleet in March 1957 and was later used extensively in the Vietnam War.

The diamond rolls and the echelon rolls and the diamond loops and the echelon loops are the basic standbys, and then you add the fleur-de-lis and that type of thing as you go along. Establish a 25- to 30-minute routine. As I say, you put in as many maneuvers as fit and keep you open in front of the crowd at the proper time. That's what you're looking for.

Q: Did you find yourself as a role model for younger Navy pilots? Were they coming to you for advice and so forth?

Captain Hawkins: Well, I don't know. Not too much, I guess. Certainly after my bailout I was well known to all the younger bucks coming through, because a flight surgeon took my taped version of the bailout, and it became required listening for all students coming through. So I was very well known from that to all the younger aviators during that time. I wouldn't be surprised if the tape is still around and still played in training every so often.

Q: I'll bet you could have heard a pin drop. This was a course on how to save your own life.

Captain Hawkins: Of course, the flight surgeons are always telling you what you did wrong: "So here's the things he did wrong. But he's alive, so here's the things he did right." There were a lot of things done wrong, no question about that.

Q: Such as?

Captain Hawkins: Such as not having a bailout oxygen bottle in the parachute I had for bailing out at high altitude. We did have the bottles. Our chutes that we left at home for this trip to pick up the airplanes had bailout bottles in them. Although in my case it wouldn't have mattered anyway, because the slipstream tore off my oxygen mask and everything when I went out. Also, since this was just supposed to be a cross-country flight, I didn't have my G-suit on. I just had my flight suit which might have saved me again, because under that I had my regular uniform on and I didn't freeze to death hanging up there at 30,000 feet, although my ears got frost-bitten. So there were lots of things that the flight surgeon could show that I did wrong, but then things he could show as doing right.

I taped this account the day after the bailout, when I returned to Corpus. So the date on the tape never changed. It was there whenever the tape was played. In fact, from that same tape a story was written for Saturday Evening Post and then later was reprinted in about 14 different countries and was picked up in books.* They don't know if it got into Russia or not, because the Russians didn't bother to pay the copyright fees.

Q: After that tour you went to General Line School in Monterey.† Was this based in part on the fact that you hadn't finished college before?

Captain Hawkins: Yes, that's true. I was taking courses all during this time. I had my two years of college when I came in, so they sent you to line school, then they sent me to Armed Forces Staff College and the Naval War College. Those were the three schools that you get if you're not in a degree program, which they did have also.

After I finished the tour in the war college, I completed my law degree from there in an after-hours program. So I finished up an L.L.B. I never did join the bar, but we had to have an advanced degree of some sort if we expected to get promoted. So everybody

---

* Lieutenant Arthur Ray Hawkins, USN, as told to Wesley Price, "I Had to Bail Out at Supersonic Speed, Saturday Evening Post, 13 March 1954, pages 32-33, 137-138. According to the article, it was the first successful bailout from a plane going faster than the speed of sound.
† For a period after World War II, the General Line School was operated at Monterey, California, and Newport, Rhode Island, to provide broad training for officers who had been commissioned in the Naval Reserve during the war and then converted to regular Navy afterward.

was going back to pick up a degree. I couldn't see picking up one in government science or something just to have one, so I went for a law degree while I was at it and got that done.

Q: What did this tour at Monterey teach you about being a better naval officer?

Captain Hawkins: Well, the line school was strictly academic. You went into advanced math, electricity. No strictly military subjects; it was all academic subjects in the line school. Now, at war college and Armed Forces Staff College it was something else. That's strictly back to your major--teaching you things on how to be a better leader. But the General Line School was strictly academic to bring you up to a college degree level. So that was completed in '54.

After that was done, I went to the VX-5, which was a special weapons test squadron where you established plans and tried all the airplanes out for delivery of your atomic weapons. You designed and published the doctrine for delivering the weapon with that particular airplane as it came out.

Q: This was at Moffett Field?

Captain Hawkins: Moffett Field and China Lake.[*] When I first joined VX-5, it was stationed at Moffett Field, but we did all of our work at China Lake, which was where all the targets were and so forth, the rake targets. A rake target is where they track you and plot your course and everything during the dive and all of this and give you a perfect mark on where your bomb hit. So we did all of our flying in China Lake. We were just home-based at Moffett. After the first year, the whole squadron moved to China Lake because we got tired of going back and forth all the time. It was much better. I mean, you're there

---

[*] China Lake Naval Ordnance Test Station, Inyokern, California.

and you can get your work done and not have to worry about moving back and forth all the time with the airplanes and the people you needed to maintain your program.

Q: What were the planes you were flying during that period?

Captain Hawkins: Well, I was running the programs for the F7U and the F9F. I also flew as a pilot in other programs that they had going. I flew in the AD in that program, and I flew the F3D, which was a twin-engine Douglas fighter which never did pan out.[*] And then I had taken over the A4D program when I received orders to command an A4D squadron.[†] Actually, then I had a six-month tour in the Pentagon before I went on to my squadron. I was called back as a technical adviser on some movies they were making. Then I went on down to Jacksonville and took over my squadron.

Q: Were these training movies?

Captain Hawkins: Yes. Admiral McCain at that time was OP-09D.[‡] He had decided they needed some movies because the aviation Navy didn't know what the submariners were doing, and the submariners didn't know what the aviators and destroyer people were doing. It was called a sea power series. We did a movie on the task force, for instance, which was the carrier part of it. These were movies that the crew of a destroyer, let's say, would see in the evening, along with the regular Hollywood movies. From seeing the task force movie out of the sea power series they felt that the destroyer people would learn what the carriers were doing, and the submariners would learn what the carriers were doing, etc., etc. So that was the idea of the films.

---

[*] F3D--Douglas Skyknight.
[†] Douglas A4D attack planes first entered the fleet in October 1956 in squadron VA-72. The A4D was 40 feet, 4 inches long, wing span of 27 feet, 6 inches, gross weight of 24,500 pounds, and top speed of 670 miles per hour.
[‡] Rear Admiral John S. McCain, Jr., USN, was director of the Progress Analysis Group in OpNav from 1955 to 1957.

We did about seven of them: one on aviation, one on submarines, one on destroyers, one on cruisers, one on minesweepers, one on the replenishment oilers, etc. We tried to cover the whole Navy spectrum where they could sort of get in bed together. That was the idea--to know what each other was doing. Not to say, "Oh, those damn people, they're not doing anything."

From there I went to command VA-46 in Cecil Field, outside of Jacksonville, Florida. We were one of the first squadrons to receive the A4Ds, so that was really why I went to Florida, I guess, because of my work on the plane in VX-5. My executive officer came from Patuxent River, where he'd had the A4D in test.[*] He was Lieutenant Commander Paul de Tamble.[†]

Q: When was this?

Captain Hawkins: August of '57. I was married in April. May was when I got to Cecil, and we got the A4Ds in about August. We had F8Fs when I got to the squadron. But we had to do our own training, because the Navy didn't have RAG squadrons at that time like they have now to break somebody in before sending him to a fleet squadron. We received some new pilots and also kept the ones that were already there flying the F8Fs. As our A4Ds came in, Paul de Tamble and I started checking the people out in the A4Ds. So we became our own RAG squadron, so to speak. We still had the F8Fs on board to keep flying while we were checking everybody out in the A4Ds.

Q: Why would the squadron convert from a fighter to attack?

Captain Hawkins: Well, really, the F8F was considered a bomber at that time because it could carry a special weapon. The A4D came in to replace that phase of aviation of the

---

[*] Naval Air Test Center, Patuxent River, Maryland.
[†] Lieutenant Commander Paul A. de Tamble, USN.

special weapons. It was the Navy's first light attack plane designed to carry the atomic bomb. So the squadron was in a fighter airplane when I got there, but it was considered a bomber squadron. It was checked out in the loft maneuvers and so forth on how to handle atomic weapons.*

Q: Could you describe what was involved in bringing the squadron up to speed with a completely new airplane?

Captain Hawkins: Well, actually you have a training syllabus which is put out by your type commander. Since we were at Jacksonville, we came under NavAirLant, which is in Norfolk.† First you check out your pilots--just getting them some time in the airplane to get used to it. From that, you take a pilot to instrument training, where he can fly the plane on instruments at night. You get your night work in so he's proficient at night in the thing.

Then you go into your weapons training. You train in bombing hops, strafing hops, whatever is required for what weapons you have on the airplane. You make him a part of a unit of four, which is called a division. You've got two sections forming a division. So you have a division leader and a section leader who are your more senior people, and two wingmen, who are your ensigns with lesser flight time. As a close-knit unit they are trained in the formation and learn to protect each other.

Your weapons training will include firing on sleeves that you are towing for gunnery proficiency. Your bombing will be on targets for bombing proficiency. Then you

---

* The loft bombing method was designed as a tactic to prevent airplanes from being damaged by their own nuclear bombs. The method called for the pilot to make a low-altitude approach to the target and pull up into the first part of a Cuban 8. The bomb would be released as the aircraft reached about 45-degree angle during the climb. The pilot then completed the half of the Cuban 8 and flew back in the direction from which he had made his approach.
† NavAirLant--Naval Air Force Atlantic Fleet.

will carqual on board ship. They have to get ten landings on board ship in a day and five at night before they're considered qualified to carqual.

When you've got that done, they should be ready. It's an ongoing process because you continually have new people coming in. Certainly in our case we had to start from scratch just about because of the brand-new airplane. It's the same syllabus, usually, but you have to go back, whereas if you have just a few people coming in--which it is when a squadron is formed and operating--you may have a turnover of a third of the pilots a year. So it's up to your divisions to bring them up as you go along in the training.

Your operations officer, who does all the scheduling and so forth, will follow the syllabus of training, which every year is then repeated. You go through it every year.

Q: You received pilots from a number of different sources--Naval Academy, ROTC, AOCS and what have you. Did you notice any differences among those groups?*

Captain Hawkins: Well, nowadays, no, you won't, because they all start in at the bottom, so to speak. They all come here and start out their flight training from scratch, so to speak. Now back in my day, during World War II, your academy people might have come into a squadron as lieutenant commanders who just got their wings. There was a little bit of a problem then, because you would have a squadron, and you may have a lieutenant (j.g.) with 2,000 hours, and you'd have a lieutenant commander show up in the squadron with only 250 hours. Well, you couldn't very well give him the experienced division leader when you've got a lieutenant (j.g.) with 2,000 hours, combat experience, and everything. So during that time it was an accepted thing to sort of forget the ranks for a while. A new pilot flew wing until he got some experience, until he felt capable of taking over leadership of a division, which his rank required as a lieutenant commander. Until he got his experience, he flew wing.

---

* ROTC--reserve officers' training corps; AOCS--aviation officer candidate school.

Of course, now you don't have that. Your academy people usually come straight from Annapolis. Because of the age limitation, you have very few that will come out of the blackshoe Navy into aviation. You may see some jaygees or maybe a lieutenant, but you won't see any lieutenant commanders or commanders coming through the program any more. You've had your choice before. In the past you didn't have your choice. They took so few that they would still give a guy a shot as lieutenant commander when he applied for the program and received his recommendations all the way through.

Q: How was it during this time in the '50s when you were a squadron CO?

Captain Hawkins: No problem there. In fact, it was the other way. We then had what we called the Holloway program.[*] A kid would go to college for two years, then he would come to the squadron, come to training, and he would fly and do a tour for three years. Then he'd go back to college to get his other two years. They came in as midshipmen--not yet commissioned. They would be midshipmen flying in your squadron. So you actually had a new thing to contend with because up until Korea, you had to be a commissioned officer to fly combat. This was mainly because if someone ended up as a POW, they wanted him to get the commissioned officers' treatment supposedly that the Geneva Conference called for.[†] So many of the enlisted pilots and aviation cadets at the start of World War II were commissioned. They were no longer APs or cadets or warrant officer pilots.[‡] They were ensigns or jaygees or whatever they promoted them to.

---

[*] In 1946, the Holloway Plan was enacted to establish a Naval ROTC program that would pay for the college education of individuals and grant regular, rather than reserve, commissions upon graduation. It was named for Rear Admiral James L. Holloway, Jr., USN, who had much to do with its development. See "A Gentlemen's Agreement," U.S. Naval Institute Proceedings, September 1980, pages 71-77.

[†] POW--prisoner of war.

[‡] AP--aviation pilot, a term to designate an enlisted naval aviator before and during World War II.

So during Korea we had midshipmen flying combat, which was a first, I assume. But by the time we had finished and all got back, they had all made jaygee on their normal tour. But when I took over VA-46, I still had three midshipmen in the squadron. They very shortly made ensigns. There was no problem there. And you didn't have the problem then of lieutenant commanders or commanders coming through the program, getting their 300 or 400 hours and reporting to the squadron. I think they had a 26-year-old limit then to enter the program, so you could bring a jaygee in and put him on the wing with no problem until he had his experience.

Q: Aside from just flying ability, how were they as all-around naval officers from these various sources?

Captain Hawkins: All in all, I would say they were compatible, whether they came from the academy or ROTC or the NavCad program or the Holloway program. Your aviation field is sort of an equalizer, I think. Let's say you have a squadron of 25 officers. It's more of a close-knit unit. Everybody has his billet to be filled. They all, I would say, were compatible. One's not hands down better or worse than the other one. I'd say your academy people have had much more training towards leadership. You get a guy from ROTC, he's had it all through his college, but then he doesn't get that drilled into him day to day to day the way they do in the academy. But it's fairly equal, I'd say.

Q: How would you describe the A4D as an airplane?

Captain Hawkins: Tinker toy. That's what they called it, but it's a fine airplane. They were looking for a cheap airplane that was simple, that they could build a lot of. But we were so set on getting into the nuclear weapons program. The Air Force almost ran away with it, and the Navy was going to be left with no mission in the nuclear program, so the airplane was redesigned to haul a special weapon. That's why the crazy long legs are under it. It's a little bitty airplane sitting up on big, tall legs, as you know. You've seen it. That was necessary to put the Fat Boy weapon on at that time. It was a huge round thing, and the plane had to sit up high for the weapon to go under it. So it was designed to carry a weight over and above its own weight.

It was a very simple airplane in the cockpit, easy to fly. You had to fly it all the time. You didn't ever let loose. It was just so small that you couldn't trim it up and say, "Okay, I'm going to sit here a while." If you had bumpy air, it'd go off in some other direction. Later they put an auto-pilot on it which helped, but still with that size of an airplane, any rough air's going to give you a problem where you're going to have to wrestle with it, if you want to call it that. We flew them night, day, in weather, and everything else. It became just the mainstay, really, of the fleet.

Q: How big a part was night flying during that time?

Captain Hawkins: Well, night flying became a firm, hard requirement during the Turkey Shoot in World War II when we all got trapped out at night and it was such a fiasco getting everybody back aboard.[*] It was just something from that time forward had to be. You had to be night qualified if you were going to be on board ship. You never knew. So it became routine once you got into it. It's just something you never did. You were night qualified when you came aboard--even World War II. We had all flown at night, and you had your five night carquals. But then that was done and you didn't bother anymore.

Then--six, seven, or eight months later--here was a requirement to come aboard after dark. From that day forward, you had to be night qualified and stay night qualified. So now the pilots have to maintain so many night landings per month so when they're on board ship they fly night and day. It's just routine now. It's not something like it used to be where you did it only when you had to. And it certainly paid off. If you can operate at

---

[*] In the first interview, Captain Hawkins talked about the air battle of 19 June 1944 off the Marianas. The following day bombers from the U.S. carriers flew west in a long tail chase of the Japanese fleet. They didn't return to their carriers until after dark and low on fuel.

night and your enemy can't, you're up and above on him already. So you have to be ready to fly in all weather, night or day.

Q: How would you describe the various roles that made up the job of a squadron CO?

Captain Hawkins: Well, during that time he was a dictator, basically. He was the judge and the jury and the leader. He had the captain's mast authority for his punishment; he could convene a court-martial. Now it's coming back to that; it went away for a while. They tried to move all the authority for punishment further up the ladder, and they found that it doesn't work. It works but not very efficiently. He was father confessor to all of his troops. And he was required to ensure that his squadron was intact to the members of the families of his troops. It was a smaller command. You're talking about 150, let's say, to 160, 170 men in a squadron. It's close-knit. It's his responsibility. If something goes wrong, it's his. That's the way it is all the way through the command. If something goes wrong, you have one guy responsible, and rightly so.

Q: Did you relish this kind of opportunity?

Captain Hawkins: Oh, yes, I enjoyed command. I lucked out through my career. Other than my few stints in the Pentagon, I was usually in a position of command from the time I was a lieutenant on forward. It just happened that way. It wouldn't ordinarily because as a senior aviator or as a lieutenant that's a command that you don't count on as a lesser rank. But in my case I did pick up command there in my unit on the cruisers. After that, I had the Blue Angel command, and from that to my squadron command, and command in the carrier air group, to my oiler. Unluckily, though, I never did get my carrier. I got a little too old. During Zumwalt's time they started requiring you to be younger to have command.* You had to be in a certain age bracket to start moving. So I ended up with my major command as the naval air station at Atsugi in Japan.

Q: As a squadron CO, do you think it helped that you had become famous through the Blue Angels and this bailout experience?

Captain Hawkins: Well, maybe, maybe not. I mean, my junior people probably were a little bit in awe: "We've got the old CO of the Blues here. He's our CO." That would wear off in a hurry, I think, but to start with I would say yes. And being in that position where we were required to train our own people gave us a little advantage. I taught them how to be "Blues."

Q: What do you remember about operations from the Franklin D. Roosevelt?†

Captain Hawkins: Well, the old Roosevelt was one of the first converted to angled deck, so she was certainly not the plush carrier that came about when they really started designing them from scratch with the angled deck. In cutting her up to put the deck on, a lot of things were not done. The staterooms were all cut up and this type of thing. But she was a fine operating ship. She was the mainstay of the Mediterranean. She must have done 20 tours over there at least. I did two and a half with her, but the operation from her was strictly peacetime. We would do our tour to the Med and back, go to training with

---

* Admiral Elmo R. Zumwalt, Jr., USN, served as Chief of Naval Operations from 1 July 1970 to 29 June 1974. He took office at age 49, the youngest ever for a CNO. He made several changes in staffing requirements, including the establishment of a "Mod Squad" of destroyers in which all the skippers were one rank junior to the norm.

† The USS Franklin D. Roosevelt was commissioned as CVB-42 on 27 October 1942. She was reclassified CVA-42 on 1 October 1952 and extensively modernized from 1954 to 1956. Among other changes, she received an enclosed hurricane bow and angled flight deck. Following the modernization she was 974 feet long, 110 feet in the beam, extreme flight deck width of 210 feet, maximum draft of 36 feet, full-load displacement of 62,000 tons, and rated speed of 33 knots. She could accommodate 70-plus aircraft.

her to the ORIs and all down around Gitmo and down in that area for that yearly training requirement.[*] Except when she was in overhaul, she was always there at Mayport for work with the air group, and we did our carquals on her.[†] When we wanted to go out, she was available to do it. But all in all, I would say for her many years at Mayport, she was in Europe or somewhere else out of port more than she was in Mayport. She was a goer.

Q: Any incidents from your time on that ship that particularly stand out?

Captain Hawkins: No, nothing. When I was air boss on the ship, we accomplished something that had never been done before. While we were on a Med tour, the steam catapults had to be peened. What this means is that the track that the shuttle ran down had expanded to a point where we were losing pressure. The steam would come out around the shuttle, and you wouldn't get a full shot. So they had to be peened.

These big pipes, if you want to call them pipes, that the cylinder went down all had to be taken out. They were peened with hammers to get them back to their proper width for the shuttle to go down. This was normally a shipyard job, but we decided with our own catapult crew that we could do it. So they let us do it. We pulled into Naples and stayed there for three weeks. We brought out two men from the naval shipyard in Philadelphia with the peening machines, and my catapult crew removed all these steam pipes, shuttle tracks, what they really are, and peened them. Doing it in the Med saved having to shuffle a ship out and replace her and go back and this type of thing.

And, of course, there were all kinds of things during peacetime that you ran into. There was a search for a lost airplane, you know, famous this and famous that, but it was just day-to-day operations.

Q: What did your job entail as air officer in the FDR?

---

[*] Gitmo--Guantanamo Bay, Cuba, was the site of operations for the fleet training group.
[†] Mayport, Florida, is near the Jacksonville Naval Air Station, where VA-46 was based.

Captain Hawkins: Well, as air boss you ran everything from the hangar deck up. You ran the airplanes in the pattern. Once the airplanes left the pattern of the ship, the ops officer and the CAG became responsible. Then the air boss became responsible again when they reported back and entered the pattern of the ship. His function was to launch them, load them, gas them. It's the ballet of the flight deck and the hangar deck, is what it amounts to. He plans the launches, how he's going to do it, how he's going to spot them, and he has to know what weapons are to be loaded, and he has to know what fuel they want on board, if they want a full load or if they want belly tanks. His is the responsibility from the hangar deck all the way up to the traffic pattern. He maintains the catapults and the arresting gear. He doesn't have to maintain the ordnance, but he has to see that it's loaded when it comes up front on the deck.

Q: How much interaction did this involve with the commanding officer, the CAG, and other top officers in the ship?

Captain Hawkins: Naturally close coordination is required, especially between the captain and the air boss. The air boss has his private telephone line, straight through to the skipper from his little bridge up on the side of the island. And he passes on questions and requirements--you know, when are they going to turn into the wind and what speed is required and wind over the deck required and this sort of thing he has to relay to the captain or the OOD who is relaying it to the captain to maintain the launch. Then the air officer has to keep the captain informed on when the deck will be respotted and be ready for this, and so on and so forth, so and so, and so and so. So close coordination is required on board ship of all department heads. They've all got to be on the same wavelength at all times. There's no other way to operate.

Q: Are there any captains that you particularly remember from that time in the various tours in that ship?

Captain Hawkins: Yes. On the Roosevelt the finest captain we had at the time I was there was Vice Admiral R. L. Shifley.* He's retired now, but he was captain then. R. L. Shifley is on the board of directors of Navy Mutual Aid, the insurance program in the Pentagon up there. He was a fine skipper.

Q: What qualities made him a fine skipper?

Captain Hawkins: Cool, understanding, delegation of responsibility, realizing he couldn't do it all himself. You've got to delegate. He passed the authority to somebody, and they knew that they had it. It wasn't a matter of, "I've got to do this for the captain." You had to do this because he had passed it to you and it was your responsibility, although he still maintained the overall responsibility. If you goofed up, he was responsible. But he trusted his people to the point of turning over responsibility to them and not trying to do it all himself.

Q: Is that a mistake carrier captains make sometimes?

Captain Hawkins: It's a mistake that a lot of commanding officers of all phases do. Sure, in a small command you can do it all yourself. But you get a carrier, there's no way. I mean, how can you sit up on the bridge and still do something that's supposed to be taking place down in the bowels of the ship? Somebody has got to have the responsibility. He can't be jumping off the bridge and running down to the engine room and telling the chief engineer to do this and do that. If he doesn't have a chief engineer that he can trust, he's

---

* Captain Ralph L. Shifley, USN, commanded the USS Franklin D. Roosevelt (CVA-42) from July 1958 to August 1959.

got to get another one. But some captains would never trust anyone. They've got to be kept up on details and details and details until finally they're just snowed under with details, and things go to pot.

On board ship the captain has got to maintain his overall responsibility, but he's got to run the ship from the bridge. His big responsibility is out from the ship. Inside the ship his responsibility is delegated to his department heads to do this and do that and see that it is done. That, to me, is the kind of skipper to have. If you make a mistake, he doesn't cut your throat. If it's something that you can square away and get right the next time, he would be there to help you do it.

Q: How much did the angled deck help you in your job of orchestrating this ballet of the flight deck?

Captain Hawkins: Oh, immensely. You could maintain a ready deck, whereas you couldn't before. You could have everything parked forward and still have a ready deck, and you could still be launching and taking more planes at the same time. With a straight deck, there was always that possibility of you trying to do both at once and a plane would come on forward into the pack. With an angled deck, unless he's really, really off center, he's not going to come into the pack; he's going to go off in the water. So it was a great improvement in the flight deck operation. A great improvement.

Q: Did the LSO work for you?[*]

Captain Hawkins: LSO worked for CAG. He was always CAG's man. Of course, now each squadron has an LSO. The CAG has an LSO also, but you operate now with a meatball, you know. It's a light which does everything that the LSO used to do, but the LSO just stands back there on the radio to talk to you if you're not paying attention to

---

[*] LSO--landing signal officer.

what the light's saying. But he's still back there, and he still has the authority to tell you to go around. But the LSO is a member of the air group.

Q: Let's move on to your job as CAG. What differences did that entail?

Captain Hawkins: Just a little more responsibility. Instead of one squadron I now had five. Five commanding officers were running their squadrons, and it was up to me to meld them into a unit, the same way you melded the divisions of your squadron. On board ship, you were directly responsible to the captain for all of them. And they were responsible to you, so the captain didn't have to deal with five different squadron commanders. He was dealing with CAG. So it's more responsibility but more of the same. The CAG had his own little staff, and he was not actually down in the day-to-day operation. His was a planning function of the total operation of the air group.

When you're back on the beach, the squadron commanders were more or less on their own for their training. The CAG would see that it was being done, but he didn't go down and say, "You will do this and this and this tomorrow." He would just see that they were following the standard training syllabus. His staff went from squadron to squadron just to check on them and see that things were being done, and through meetings and understandings, he kept them melded together on the beach. But when they came aboard ship, they really became a unit. The CAG was in the overall planning of operations--assigning the operations to the squadrons as they came from the admiral to the ship to the air group commander. Then the squadrons did their own assigning of pilots to accomplish the functions that the CAG had passed to them to do. But if something went wrong, the commanding officer of the ship called the CAG; he didn't call the squadron commander.

On the beach, your command judicial punishment was with the COs of the squadrons and the CAG. But once you went aboard ship, the thing just moved up to the captain of the ship. He then was the only one with the authority to convene court-martials and what have you. The COs would have their own non-judicial punishment within the group, but as far as court-martials, only the CO of the ship could convene those. The CO also took over all leave policy and those types of things that on the beach are back with the CAG. When you were on board, it moved up one notch.

Q: Is air group commander the best job a carrier pilot can have?

Captain Hawkins: Well, it's the ultimate for a pilot. You've gone up the ladder then when you hit CAG. That's the last flying job, really. I mean, that's in the plan. From then on it's department head jobs and so forth. You've made commander, so that's your last flying job.

Q: What were your duties in the air?

Captain Hawkins: Actually, your duty in the air would be only if you determined that you were going into the air for an overall mission. Let's say you've got your bombers and your fighters going on one strike. The CAG may go as the overall coordinator for the entire strike, or he may designate a squadron commander. He doesn't go on all of them. So your senior squadron commander becomes the strike commander for another large flight. So that is the only function he will be in the air as a strike commander on a flight that he has taken. It's up to him then to designate who it will be on a flight. On most of them with the special weapons, you didn't run into this, because it involved only one, two, three planes. The pilot himself was more or less the strike commander. He took it, and he was gone. The coordination was done before he left. In World War II it wasn't uncommon for a flight of 200 airplanes to go up together, all on one mission, and you had a strike commander. It was usually one of the CAGs from the ships they had come from, a senior man, or whoever the admiral had designated that the strike commander would be that day. He was the in-air, on-scene commander on all the flights.

Q: Interspersed with these various squadron and shipboard jobs, you went to the Naval War College and the Armed Forces Staff College. What can you say about those tours?

Captain Hawkins: Well, the Armed Forces Staff College is a joint college where you've got Army, Navy, and Air Force all together in classes. It's basically a Joint Chiefs of Staff school. They formed it themselves for that reason--to get the services working together. At that school you were supposed to learn joint operations, how the Joint Chiefs worked at the Pentagon, how everything was done. That basically was the thought behind it.

And, of course, the Naval War College is just that. It's a place that you're supposed to go as a fairly senior officer. As the old thing used to say, "to contemplate better ways to improve the way the Navy operates." Well, it's gone a little farther than that now. Used to, that was it. They'd go there, and they'd write a thesis on this or a thesis on that and be more or less on their own to do these things. Well, that's not the case anymore. When you go there now, you have an established curriculum you follow. You know you're going to study tactics one day, and you know you're going to shipboard this and shipboard that the next day and you'll go through these things. Then, to cover the contemplative part, they bring in experts on different subjects--civilians, the economy, or whatever--to talk to seminars and this type of thing. You still are required to determine what thesis you're going to write on, and your whole nine months there, you're operating and working on this one thesis. It should be something new, a new thought, how to do something different. Through your studies and research and so forth, try to come up with something so that you left the school with something that was worthwhile.

Q: What was it in your case?

Captain Hawkins: I did a thesis on program planning. Those were the years when McNamara was just getting started.* I came in with McNamara and lived with him through it. I was working in that area, so I did my thesis on program planning. It was one of the six selected for the year to be presented to the class, so I had to present my thesis at the end of the year from the stage with all hands in attendance. It went off fairly well.

Q: What conclusions did you come up with?

Captain Hawkins: Well, eventually the system was good. I mean, the five-year program planning system as originally envisioned was very good. You just could not do it in isolation down in OSD.† It had to be done with some delegation back down to the services, the same old thing we've talked about for years and years and years. If you want a dictator, have one. If you don't, you've got to listen to your people. You can't just say, "The Navy's asking for four million dollars. They don't need it." You've got to think, "Well, they must need it or they wouldn't ask for it." And so you find out what is needed, rather than just saying, "They're just asking for it, hoping to get something."

But as far as the five-year plan ahead, that had never been done before. It was always done budget by budget by budget. So McNamara did do one good thing when he put the five-year planning system in. It is still there. It's been modified quite drastically now, but still the same principle of long-range planning, which they'd never had until he came in. They did, but it wasn't anything official. When you start building ships, you've got to have a long-range plan because it takes so long to build them. But every year it was budget by budget. If you got the budget, you'd build them. If you didn't get it, you didn't get it. So under McNamara you got five approved instead of just for that one budget. So you got five approved to put them in the program, and you got the budget as you went along, or you tried to get the budget.

---

* Robert S. McNamara served as Secretary of Defense from 21 January 1961 to 29 February 1968.
† OSD--Office of the Secretary of Defense.

Q: Of course, the fallacy in that is that there's sort of a subconscious thing, "Well, we'll get that in the 'out' years." And the "out" years never come.

Captain Hawkins: Right. Well, still, it's better to say, "The plan is I want five of these, and I can spread them out," instead of saying, "Put these five in the budget right now," which doesn't mean you're going to get it out there, but at least you're planning on getting it. And you do have a plan to ask for it the next budget next year, whereas you're not saying, "I need five of these this year and I won't have any more the rest of the year. I'll buy something else next year." The system was sound. It's just the way they went about it, they got people making the decisions that didn't have the slightest idea what they were making decisions about.

For instance, being right in the program, I can tell you some fallacies of it. When we brought the battlewagon out during Vietnam, OSD wanted it as cheap as they could.[*] So they wanted to man it with a minimum of people required to do the job. So this was all done down in isolation, by the thinkers down below:

"Okay, we're going to have a main battery."

"Yes."

"Okay, there are five 5-inch gun mounts down one side and five 5-inch gun mounts down the other side. We need all those functional."

"No, we just need one side functional. So we'll just get enough people to be able to fire the 5-inch guns on one side, and then when the ship reverses course, they can go over and man the ones on the other side."

That was well and good, except that when you're in battle stations, there's no way to get from this side to that side. You've got to go down in the bowels of the ship, break

---

[*] The USS New Jersey (BB-62) was recommissioned in April 1968 for Vietnam service and then decommissioned again in December 1969.

condition zebra, go all the way across, and get on that side.* But done in isolation, that looked like a good cost-saving thing. Just put enough people to man the 5-inch guns down one side. That was one of the stupid things they did. It was hard to get back to them to convince them you couldn't do that, it wasn't possible.

Q: Another factor in that situation was that the CNO didn't want the battleship at all.[†]

Captain Hawkins: That's true too.
  I was there for two full tours in program planning.

Q: Was this an outgrowth of your thesis?

Captain Hawkins: Well, no. More or less I went to the program planning when McNamara did. I showed up in early '61, when he came in. I went into the program planning shop in the SecNav's office because they didn't have any aviators in there and they had to have some aviators in there.[‡] So two of us showed up as program planners, which was from scratch, teaching ourselves from then on. So after my first tour in that, I went to the war college, wrote my thesis, and then came back. Actually, I went from the war college to my oiler, but I got to keep the oiler for only nine months, because they wanted me back in the Pentagon for the same shop that I had come out of.

Q: Did your office in program planning work with the OPA, the Office of Program Appraisal?

---

* Condition zebra is a maximum condition of watertight integrity, with hatches and watertight doors closed and thus precluding movement inside the ship.
† Admiral David L. McDonald, USN, served as Chief of Naval Operations from 1 August 1963 to 1 August 1967.
‡ SecNav--Secretary of the Navy.

Captain Hawkins: Yes.

Q: Was Admiral Kauffman there during that time?*

Captain Hawkins: Yes.

Q: What do you remember about him?

Captain Hawkins: Not too much. I really don't. We were fully taken up, let's put it that way. We worked from 6:00 in the morning until 9:00, 10:00, 11:00 at night every day, sometimes Sundays during that time. We had formed the PEC, the Program Evaluation Center, for SecNav up in our office. And we were running the PEC. I had nine GS-15s that were program analysts. And day in, day out, McNamara's questions would come up, and we had to have the answer at 6:00 o'clock the next morning when he came in. He'd leave at 6:00 at night, throw them on the desk, and by the time they filtered up, we'd get them at 9:00 o'clock at night, and they'd want them answered by 6:00 in the morning. So that was the cycle he was under then.

No, I knew Draper not too well, but I knew him and spoke to him and was in meetings with him and so forth. In fact, the OPA was the SecNav's alter ego for talking to Enthoven downstairs, is what it amounted to.† Then through a study that they pulled me back for--that's what they pulled me back for from my ship--we set up OP-96, which was the same as OPA when OPA came into it.

Q: OP-96 was systems analysis division.

---

* Rear Admiral Draper L. Kauffman, USN, whose oral history is in the Naval Institute collection.
† Alain C. Enthoven served as Deputy Comptroller and Deputy Assistant Secretary of Defense, 1961-65, and as Assistant Secretary of Defense for Systems Analysis, 1965-69.

Captain Hawkins: Systems analysis division that Zumwalt took over as a captain, and later he made admiral. He was frocked up there. I had done the study to set that up, because CNO had no one to talk to Enthoven. He needed somebody that they would accept as, "Yes, those analysts we can talk to them." So that was established, and I was still running the program down in OP-90.* OP-90 was the SecNav center to try to keep up with things. We published the five-year program and all that out of there and did all the work.

But I lived through the full McNamara reign from start to finish.

Q: Is that when the gray hair started coming?

Captain Hawkins: That's right--and the bifocals. That's exactly when they came. I got the bifocals right out of that Pentagon office where the lights were about 12 feet up to the ceiling. That got to my eyes, I guess.

Q: Let's touch on your tour in the Caloosahatchee.† What do you remember about that time?

Captain Hawkins: Well, I loved it. It was completely different from anything I was used to as an aviator, although I had had my shipboard duty, of course, as air boss and everything. I was still qualified for operating a ship. I reported aboard as a captain, and I found that my next senior officer was a lieutenant commander. I got a little itch of the thing, wondering, "Well, how does this go?" And then I looked at the rest of my officers.

---

* OP-90--the General Programming Division in the extended staff of the Chief of Naval Operations.
† Captain Hawkins was commanding officer from 6 August 1965 to 23 April 1966. The USS Caloosahatchee (AO-98) was commissioned on 10 October 1945. She was 553 feet long, 75 feet in the beam, had a draft of 32 feet, and displaced 25,440 tons fully loaded. She had a top speed of 18 knots and a cargo capacity of more than six million gallons of fuel oil. In the late 1960s she was "jumboized" to give her an even greater capacity.

After the lieutenant commander was perhaps one lieutenant, because for some reason that's when they start getting out, I guess. But then they dropped down even more. So mostly I had a bunch of jaygees and a bunch of ensigns.

Q: A real leadership challenge.

Captain Hawkins: You think, "Well, I've got to find out what kind of warrants and chiefs I've got on this outfit." I dropped down one more notch and checked out the warrants. Usually that's where your oilers and your service force ships live and die--on your warrants and your chiefs. Luckily, I had two or three good ones, a boatswain and a fuel king, and some real fine chiefs. Of course, my exec was a crackerjack. He was named Mullaney and was a graduate of the Merchant Marine Academy.[*]

The ship was based in Newport in ServRon 2.[†] ServRon 2 was down in Norfolk, but Caloosahatchee was in Newport, which was fine, in my case, because in Newport for training you didn't have to bother going out of the Chesapeake Bay for 40 miles to get out. You got permission to leave the dock, and you left the dock, and you went out and trained, and you came back in at night if you wanted to come in or stay out if you wanted. You were pretty much your own boss, which helped, because I could do the training that I felt I needed and not have to have a commodore breathing down my back all the time while I was getting squared away. So I took over the ship in Newport, and it couldn't have been a finer tour. I just enjoyed it immensely.

We deployed a couple of times. We went to the Med, but we only stayed enough to do some fueling and came back. As the commanding officer of the Caloosahatchee, I ended up with the task force for the Gemini 8 landing. I had three destroyers and the "Caloos." It was supposed to land in the Atlantic, but it had troubles and it landed in the

---

[*] Lieutenant Commander Robert E. Mullaney, USN.
[†] ServRon 2--Service Squadron Two.

Pacific.* So we really didn't get to pick it up, but I had the force for where it was supposed to land. And if the space capsule didn't make that point, it would hit just off the tip of Africa. So we were equipped with communications. We'd talk to the Geminis, and they'd go over and check them out, let them know we were there and all this. They ended up with some problems and had to splash down in the Pacific, so we didn't get to pick them up.

But during that tour down off the tip of Africa, we had one exciting event. A merchant ship caught on fire. It was on the Danish line carrying cotton, wheat, and wool from South America. They put out a "May Day" distress call, and back from our headquarters in Washington came the word to assist them. They were a distance away from us. I detached the three destroyers. They could go much faster than I could. I could only do 15 knots, and those destroyers could do 30. I detached them immediately to go and render assistance as they could, and we would follow. So they did.

They got there the day before we did. The fire was burning in the hull of the ship. All this baled wool had caught fire from a cigarette, probably, when the stevedores put it on. It was burning inside, and there was no way you could put it out. They wanted to abandon ship. So I went over, and we went aboard and talked with the CO. He wanted to try to save his ship. Of course, you know they have a cargo master on board those things that owns the cargo. The captain of the ship was supposed to run the ship. The cargo master--that's his cargo. Well, we told him that if he wanted to save the ship we'd have to dump some of that over the side. "Oh, no, not my cargo."

"Okay, let it burn up, and you won't have any cargo." So then it became the captain's decision. It was his ship. He had to make the decision. His crew was ready to come on and get on our ship. They weren't doing a thing except sitting around. So we went back

---

* The Gemini 8 space capsule was launched on 16 March 1966, manned by two astronauts, civilian Neil A. Armstrong and Major David R. Scott, USAF. The plan was to make 44 earth orbits, but mechanical malfunctions cut the mission to seven orbits. On 17 March the capsule came down in a designated secondary landing near Okinawa and was recovered by the destroyer Leonard F. Mason (DD-852).

and established a fire-fighting detail. The exec went over with them to survey the situation. He found that one crane on the whole ship worked. They had 22 winches, and only one of them worked. So our first order of business was the electrician to put all the cranes back in shape. Our electricians got 12 cranes operating fairly fast. So the crew I had over there started bringing these bales of wool out over the side. We fought that fire for three days, put it out, launched the guy on his merry way. So about the most exciting thing that happened to us on the Caloosahatchee was operating with the merchant fleet. It was really something. We finally got the crew to get off their duffs and assist, after they saw we were going to put the fire out. They got busy and helped out. We ran a shuttle boat back and forth daily with a new crew.

Q: How long did all this take?

Captain Hawkins: It took three days to get that hull emptied and down into where the wool--we threw over all of it that was burning. Down below the wool were coffee beans. If those ever caught, they'd still be burning today. But we got it out and he made it on in to Dakar, and they went on in to Africa.

Q: Typically that is the deep-draft command that precedes the carrier command, and you said you lost out on that. Did that cause you any bitterness?

Captain Hawkins: I would have loved to have a carrier, yes. No doubt about that. That's the goal of every aviator--to have his own carrier. But there's only so many. During my time we only had 12 of them.

Q: It was more a policy change that caught you.

Captain Hawkins: Oh, yes. During that time there was a big policy change. Ages dropped for flag command, for flag rank, all kinds of changes during the Zumwalt years when everything was in complete change. So they established age limits for this and this and that. It was just a matter of being at the wrong place at the wrong time, but I wasn't bitter. No, no. I enjoyed my tour in Japan as my final command.

Q: Let's touch on that, then.

Captain Hawkins: I was assigned to Naval Air Station Atsugi, which is our only naval air station in Japan. It was a master jet base at that time. On the base we had Nippon Aircraft Company. They did all of our overhaul and maintenance work for all the airplanes coming out of Vietnam. Planes would come in, and we would put them through rework in the Japanese plant. We did all the engine work and all the confidential work on radars and so forth on the air base side. All my people did that. Then they'd mate them together, and back would go a new airplane to Vietnam. It was a great savings of money because once you picked up an airplane, sent it back to the States, repaired it, sent it back to Vietnam, it was costing you about ten times as much as we were able to do it with Japanese labor. And they were fantastic. Their motto was, "Give us an airplane with a bureau number on it, and we'll repair it for you." And that was about true. I've seen three and four helicopters come in, Marine helicopters, just pieces here and there and there. And out of the three, they'd build one perfect one.

Q: How did the planes get there?

Captain Hawkins: Bring them in by ship or bring them in by the big helos. They'd come into Yokosuka or one of the ports. We were inland a little ways. The big crane helos would bring them over, or they would come over by truck, bus, any way we could get them there. But some of them would fly in. They had put in their 2,500-3,000 hours or whatever on the engine, and they'd bring them in for a PAR--preventive aircraft maintenance, it's called. Aircraft rework.

Q: What sort of relationship did you have with the aircraft carriers?

Captain Hawkins: The carriers would come in at Yokosuka, and the air groups would come on up to Atsugi. They'd fly off before the carrier went into port. Then the aircraft would train out of Atsugi all the time when the ship was in port. So that was, to me, a gratifying tour, really. Admiral Riera, whom you talked to yesterday, was my admiral on board out there.* He was ComFAirWestPac, one of the tenants on the base. Here was Emmett, who was an old World War II aviator, and here was I, the great Jap killer, and I got a little uncomfortable about this.

Q: He said he made some good friends there.

Captain Hawkins: I'll tell you, it was just fantastic. Actually, they wanted to talk about the war. We would give these cocktail parties, and you always ended up with some guy who would want to know, "Where were you? Were you here or there or there?" And he'd say, "I was shot down at so-and-so," or, "I shot somebody down in so-and-so." I couldn't have had a better relationship with them than I did. In fact, when it was time for me to leave, the four mayors in the outlying areas of my base wrote a letter to Admiral Moorer, who was the Chairman of the Joint Chiefs of Staff.† They wanted me to stay. They didn't want me to leave. I said, "All the medals I got for shooting down Japanese, and then the Japanese gave me a medal when I left Japan. I cherish that more than anything."

Q: That's a good windup for your career and a good windup for our interview.

---

* Rear Admiral R. Emmett Riera, USN, was Commander Fleet Air Western Pacific.
† Admiral Thomas H. Moorer, USN, served as Chairman of the Joint Chiefs of Staff from 3 July 1970 to 30 June 1974. His oral history is in the Naval Institute collection.

Captain Hawkins: That's where she stops, right there.

Q: Thank you very much.

Index To

Reminiscences of

Captain Arthur R. Hawkins

U.S. Navy (Retired)

A4D Skyhawk
Flown by Attack Squadron 46 in the late 1950s, 75-76; designed for nuclear weapons delivery, 75, 79-80

A6M Zero
Mitsubishi-built Japanese fighter plane that demonstrated great maneuverability during World War II air actions, 5-6, 23-24

Air Force, U.S.
Conducted bombing runs from Japan during the Korean War, 53-54; during the Korea War the Air Force operated a joint center that coordinated bombing targets for U.S. aircraft, 60-61; a pilot was killed in the early 1950s when he bailed out of his F-86 at faster than the speed of sound, 67

Air Group 31
Began workup training at Atlantic City, New Jersey, in 1943, 12-13; reported to the aircraft carrier Cabot (CVL-28) in the summer of 1943, 13-15; had a long combat deployment in 1944, 16-31; between combat tours, the air group trained at Hollister, California, in 1944-45, 32-35; pilots from the air group enjoyed liberty in San Francisco in the spring of 1945, 33-34; deployed on board the aircraft carrier Belleau Wood (CVL-24) for the final months of the war against Japan in 1945, 35-38

Alcohol
Captain William O. Gallery, USN, commanding officer of the aircraft carrier Princeton (CV-37) during the Korean War, distributed beer to pilots and crew members, 55-56

Army Air Forces, U.S.
Pilot Alva Guy Hawkins was killed by the Japanese while flying near Port Moresby in 1942, 1; mock dogfights against Navy pilots in 1945, 35; B-29 bombers overflew the battleship Missouri (BB-63) in Tokyo Bay following the Japanese surrender in September 1945, 37

Astronauts
The Gemini 8 space capsule was not able to go to its primary recovery area in the Atlantic in March 1966 because of mechanical problems, 95-96

Atlantic City (New Jersey) Naval Air Station
Went into commission in 1943 to prepare naval aviators for aircraft carrier duty, 12-13

Atsugi (Japan) Naval Air Station
Did a considerable amount of aircraft overhaul and repair work during the late 1960s, 98-99

Attack Squadron 46 (VA-46)
Converted from F8Fs to A4Ds in 1957, 75-76; training in nuclear weapons delivery, 76-77, 79-80; commissioning sources for pilots in the squadron in the late 1950s, 77-79; role of Hawkins as commanding officer, 81; operations from the aircraft carrier Franklin D. Roosevelt (CVA-42), 82-83

B-29 Superfortress
Dozens of these Army Air Forces bombers overflew the battleship Missouri (BB-63) in Tokyo Bay following the Japanese surrender in September 1945, 37

Belleau Wood, USS (CVL-24)
Skipper William G. Tomlinson had an interesting nickname while commanding the ship in 1945, 18; hit by a Japanese kamikaze in October 1944, 32; had Air Group 31 on board for the final months of the war against Japan in 1945, 35-38

Blue Angels
Navy demonstration flight team switched from F6F Hellcats to F8F Bearcats to jets in the late 1940s, 45-48; air show routines, 47-49, 70-71; qualification process for the team, 49-50; formed the nucleus of Fighter Squadron 191 when it was established for Korean War duty in 1950, 50-51; flew F9F-5s and F9F-6s in the early 1950s, 64-72; Hawkins ejected from the cockpit of an F9F-6 Cougar in August 1953, 66-69, 71-72

Bombing
Training and practice by newly commissioned naval aviators in 1943, 6-7; use of F6F Hellcats for bombing during World War II, 18-20; U.S. F6F Hellcats attacked and sank the Japanese battleship Ike in July 1945, 35-36; done by F9F Panthers flying from the aircraft carrier Princeton (CV-37) during the Korean War, 52-55, 59-60; the A4D Skyhawk was designed in the 1950s for the delivery of nuclear weapons, 76-77, 79-80

Bonin Islands
U.S. carrier plane strikes against the islands in the summer of 1944, 27-28

Budgetary Matters
Secretary Robert S. McNamara introduced five-year budgeting to the Department of Defense in the early 1960s, 90-91; DoD attempts to save money in the reactivation of the battleship New Jersey (BB-62) in the late 1960s, 91-92; role of the Office of Program Appraisal, 92-94

Cabot, USS (CVL-28)
Went into commission in the summer of 1943 and took aboard Air Group 31 for training, 13; comparison with the carriers of the Essex (CV-9) class, 15-16; well-known officers in the ship's company during World War II, 17; skippers during World War II, 17-18; combat operations with Air Group 31 in 1944, 18-31; remained in combat even after her initial air group departed, 32

Caloosahatchee, USS (AO-98)
Fleet oiler that operated with few experienced officers in the mid-1960s, 94-95; routine operations out of Newport, 95; was part of the task force originally scheduled to recover astronauts in the Gemini 8 space flight in March 1966, 95-96; was part of a group that helped put out a fire on board a merchant ship burning off Africa in the mid-1960s, 96-97

Catapults
Ship's force repairs to the steam catapults in the aircraft carrier Franklin D. Roosevelt (CVA-42) in the late 1950s, 83

Charger, USS (CVE-30)
Escort carrier used for qualification training of newly commissioned naval aviators in 1943, 7-9

China, People's Republic of
U.S. aircraft were not permitted beyond North Korea into Communist China during the Korean War, 59-60

Commercial Ships
Hawkins and a friend rode a freighter from Eniwetok to Panama in 1945, following the end of World War II, 38-39; the oiler Caloosahatchee (AO-98) was part of a group that helped put out a fire on board a merchant ship burning off Africa in the mid-1960s, 96-97

Corpus Christi (Texas) Naval Air Station
Site of flight training for naval aviation cadets in 1942, 2-3

Dallas (Texas) Naval Air Station
Site of flight training for naval aviation cadets in 1942, 2

Damage Control
The oiler Caloosahatchee (AO-98) was part of a group that helped put out a fire on board a merchant ship burning off Africa in the mid-1960s, 96-97

Defense Department
Secretary Robert S. McNamara introduced five-year budgeting to DoD in the early 1960s, 90-91; DoD attempts to save money in the reactivation of the battleship New Jersey (BB-62) in the late 1960s, 91-92; role of the Office of Program Appraisal, 92-94

de Tamble, Lieutenant Commander Paul D., USN
Served as executive officer of Attack Squadron 46 in the late 1950s, 75

Education
The Navy's General Line School covered academic subjects in the mid-1950s, 72-73

Ejection Seats
Hawkins ejected from an F9F-6 Cougar in August 1953, the first pilot to eject through the canopy, 66-69, 71-72

Essex (CV-9) Class
Comparisons with light carriers such as the Cabot (CVL-28) in World War II, 15-17

Experimental Squadron Five (VX-5)
Tested a variety of new aircraft in the mid-1950s, 70, 73-74

F2A Buffalo
Brewster-built fighter plane used for operational training of newly commissioned naval aviators in 1943, 3, 6

F6F Hellcat
Grumman-built fighter that was also used as a bomber by Fighter Squadron 31 during the U.S. island-hopping campaign in 1944, 18-31; handling characteristics, 20, 23-24; used for hijinks while VF-31 was in training in early 1945, 34-35

F8F Bearcat
Grumman-built fighter flown by the Blue Angels flight demonstration team in the late 1940s, 45-49; was flown by Attack Squadron 46 in the late 1950s until replaced by A4Ds, 75-76

F9F-2/5 Panther
　Grumman-built jet fighter flown by the Blue Angels flight demonstration team in 1949-50, 46-48; flown by VF-191 from the aircraft carrier Princeton (CV-37) during the Korean War, 51-64; used by the Blue Angels until 1953, 64-65

F9F-6 Cougar
　Grumman-built jet fighter flown by the Blue Angels flight demonstration team in the mid-1950s, 65-72; first flying-tail aircraft flown by the Navy, 65-66; Hawkins ejected from the cockpit of a Cougar in August 1953, 66-69, 71-72

F-86 Sabre
　An Air Force pilot was killed in the early 1950s when he bailed out of his F-86 at faster than the speed of sound, 67

Fighter Director Officers
　Role in coaching U.S. carrier-based fighter planes during air combat in the Pacific in World War II, 29-30

Fighter Squadron 31 (VF-31)
　Began workup training at Atlantic City, New Jersey, in 1943, 12-13; reported to the aircraft carrier Cabot (CVL-28) in the summer of 1943, 13-15; had a long combat deployment in 1944, 16-31; between combat tours, the squadron trained at Hollister, California, in 1944-45, 32-35; mock dogfights against Army pilots, 35; deployed on board the aircraft carrier Belleau Wood (CVL-24) for the final months of the war against Japan in 1945, 35-38

Fighter Squadron 191 (VF-191)
　Formed in 1950 around a nucleus from the Blue Angels, 50-51; operations from the aircraft carrier Princeton (CV-37) during the Korean War, 51-64

Fires
　The oiler Caloosahatchee (AO-98) was part of a group that helped put out a fire on board a merchant ship burning off Africa in the mid-1960s, 96-97

Flight Training
　For aviation cadets in Texas in 1942, 2; operational training in Florida for newly commissioned aviators in 1943, 4-8; attrition rate in training, 9-10; preflight training to establish a pool of potential trainees during World War II, 11-12; in 1946 former fighter pilots were retrained to fly battleship and cruiser floatplanes, 40

Franklin D. Roosevelt, USS (CVA-42)
　Aircraft carrier that made frequent deployments to the Mediterranean in the 1950s, 82-83; ship's force repairs to the steam catapults in the late 1950s, 83; flight deck operations, 84, 86-87; Captain Ralph Shifley was an excellent skipper in the late 1950s, 85

Gallery, Captain William O., USN (USNA, 1925)
　Was popular with his crew while commanding the aircraft carrier Princeton (CV-37) during the Korean War, 55-57

Gemini 8
　Space capsule that was not able to go to its primary recovery area in the Atlantic in March 1966 because of mechanical problems, 95-96

General Line School, Monterey, California
Provided education in academic subjects in the mid-1950s, 72-73

Guam, Marianas Islands
Used as a base by Japanese aircraft during the U.S. invasion of Saipan in June 1944, 21-23

Hawkins, Captain Arthur Ray, USN (Ret.)
Education of, 1; brother of, 1; experience as a private pilot, 1, 4; training as a naval aviation cadet and new naval aviator in 1942-43, 2-12; service in Fighter Squadron 31 during World War II, 12-38; return to the United States and civilian life following the end of the war, 38-40; headed the floatplane detachment in the light cruiser Portsmouth (CL-102), 1946-48, 40-45; service in the Blue Angels flight demonstration team, 1948-50, 45-50; service in Fighter Squadron 191 during the Korean War, 50-64; commanded the Blue Angels in the early 1950s, 64-72; service from 1954 to 1956 in Experimental Squadron Five, 70; studied at the General Line School for six months in 1954, 72-73; commanded Attack Squadron 46 in 1957-58, 75-83; served 1958-60 as air officer of the aircraft carrier Franklin D. Roosevelt (CVA-42), 83-87; served as Commander Carrier Air Group One in 1960-61, 87-88; as a student at the Naval War College in the early 1960s, 89-90; commanded the oiler Caloosahatchee (AO-98) in 1965-66, 94-97; commanded the U.S. Naval Air Station, Atsugi, Japan, 1968-70, 98-99

Hollister, California
Site of training for Carrier Air Group 31 in 1944-45, 32-35

Ise (Japanese Battleship)
U.S. F6F Hellcats attacked and sank the ship at Kure, Japan in July 1945, 35-36

Iwo Jima, Bonin Islands
U.S. carrier plane strikes against the island in the summer of 1944, 27-28

J2M "Jack" (Japanese Fighter Plane)
Fought against U.S. Navy F6F Hellcats late in World War II, 37

"Jack"
See J2M "Jack" (Japanese Fighter Plane)

Japan
Overflight of U.S. carrier planes following the Japanese surrender on board the battleship Missouri (BB-63) in Tokyo Bay September 1945, 37; the Atsugi Naval Air Station did a considerable amount of aircraft overhaul and repair work during the late 1960s, 98-99

Japanese Navy
Attacked by U.S. Navy aircraft at Truk Atoll in early 1944, 19-21; air combat against U.S. fighters during the invasion of Saipan in June 1944, 21-23; during the campaign in the Philippines in the autumn of 1944, 24-26, 30-31; doctrine for scouting, 29-31; U.S. F6F Hellcats attacked and sank the Japanese battleship Ise in July 1945, 35-36

Ki 43 "Oscar" (Japanese Fighter Plane)
Dogfights against U.S. Navy aircraft around the Philippine Islands in the autumn of 1944, 25-26

Korean War
The Blue Angels demonstration flight team formed the nucleus of Fighter Squadron 191 when it was established for Korean War duty in 1950, 50-51; operations of VF-191 from the aircraft carrier Princeton (CV-37), 51-64; the Air Force operated a joint center that coordinated bombing targets for U.S. aircraft, 60-61; limited air threat against U.S. forces, 61-62; difficult weather conditions for aircraft operations, 62-63

Kure, Japan
U.S. F6F Hellcats attacked and sank the Japanese battleship Ise in July 1945, 35-36

Kwajalein Atoll, Marshall Islands
Role of Air Group 31 and the aircraft carrier Cabot (CVL-28) during the U.S. invasion in early 1944, 18-19

Leave and Liberty
Pilots from Air Group 32 enjoyed liberty in San Francisco in the spring of 1945, 33-34

Magda, Lieutenant Commander John J., USN
Was shot down and killed while commanding Fighter Squadron 191 during the Korean War, 65-66

Marianas Islands
Role of Air Group 31 and the aircraft carrier Cabot (CVL-28) during the U.S. invasion in June 1944, 21-23

Marshall Islands
Role of Air Group 31 and the aircraft carrier Cabot (CVL-28) during the U.S. invasion in early 1944, 18-19

McCain, Rear Admiral John S., Jr., USN (USNA, 1931)
Was in charge in the mid-1950s when OpNav made training films to provide naval personnel with a broader knowledge of their service, 74-75

McNamara, Robert S.
Introduced five-year budgeting to the Department of Defense in the early 1960s, 90-91; placed heavy demands on the DoD staff, 93

Medical Problems
The physical requirements were quite strenuous for candidates going into naval aviation training early in World War II, 9-11

Miami (Florida) Naval Air Station
Site of operational training for newly commissioned naval aviators in 1943, 4-7

Missouri, USS (BB-63)
Overflight of U.S. carrier planes during the Japanese surrender on 2 September 1945, 37

Motion Pictures
In the mid-1950s OpNav made training films to provide naval personnel with a broader knowledge of their service, 74-75

Murphy, Lieutenant Francis J., USN
Flew as part of the Blue Angels flight demonstration team both before and after service in the Korean War, 64-65

N2S Kaydet
Stearman trainer used for flight training of naval aviation cadets in 1942, 2-3

Naval Academy, Annapolis, Maryland
As a commissioning source for naval aviators who served in the 1940s and 1950s, 77-79

Naval Ordnance Test Station, Inyokern, California
Provided the base of operations for Experimental Squadron Five in the mid-1950s, 73-74

Naval Reserve
Performance of reserve pilots recalled for active duty in Navy carrier squadrons during World War II, 58-59

Naval War College, Newport, Rhode Island
During his time as a student in the early 1960s, Hawkins wrote a thesis on Navy program planning, 89-90

New Jersey, USS (BB-62)
Department of Defense attempts to save money in the reactivation of the ship (BB-62) in the late 1960s, 91-92

Night Flying
In World War II U.S. aircraft carrier operations, night flying was highly unusual; subsequently it became routine for Navy pilots, 80-81

North Korea
U.S. aircraft were not permitted beyond North Korea into Communist China during the Korean War, 59-60

Nuclear Weapons
The A4D Skyhawk was designed in the 1950s for the delivery of nuclear weapons, 76-77, 79-80

Office of Program Appraisal
Role in evaluating Navy budgetary matters in the 1960s, 92-94

"Oscar"
See Ki 43 "Oscar" (Japanese Fighter Plane)

Panama
Hawkins and a friend stopped for a time in Panama while making their way back to the United States from the Pacific in 1945, 38-39

Philippine Islands
Air actions in support of the U.S. invasion in the autumn of 1944, 24-27, 30-31

Portsmouth, USS (CL-102)
Light cruiser that operated SC-1 Seahawk floatplanes in the late 1940s, 41-43; relations between aviators and the ship's company officers, 43-44; Mediterranean cruises in the late 1940s, 44-45

Princeton, USS (CV-37)
Aircraft carrier that was reactivated from mothballs in 1950 for service in the Korean War, 51-64

Radar
Used by fighter director officers in coaching U.S. carrier-based fighter planes during air combat in the Pacific in World War II, 29-30

Rescue at Sea
The oiler Caloosahatchee (AO-98) was part of a group that helped put out a fire on board a merchant ship burning off Africa in the mid-1960s, 96-97

SC-1 Seahawk
Curtiss-built floatplane that flew from the light cruiser Portsmouth (CL-102) in the late 1940s, 41-43

SNJ Texan
North American-built plane used for advanced training of naval aviation cadets in 1942, 4, 6-7

Saipan, Marianas Islands
Role of Air Group 31 and the aircraft carrier Cabot (CVL-28) during the U.S. invasion in June 1944, 21-23

San Francisco, California
Pilots from Air Group 32 enjoyed liberty in San Francisco in the spring of 1945, 33-34

Shifley, Captain Ralph L., USN (USNA, 1933)
Did an excellent job as skipper of the aircraft carrier Franklin D. Roosevelt (CVA-42) in 1958-59, 85

Space Program
The Gemini 8 space capsule was not able to go to its primary recovery area in the Atlantic in March 1966 because of mechanical problems, 95-96

Tactics
The Thach Weave was a fighter plane tactic developed for use against the Japanese in World War II, 5-6; use of the loft method in the 1950s to practice delivery of nuclear weapons, 76

Thach Weave
Fighter plane tactic developed for use against the Japanese in World War II, 5-6, 23-24, 26

Tomlinson, Captain William G., USN (USNA, 1920)
Had the nickname "Air Medal Tomlinson" while commanding the aircraft carrier Belleau Wood (CVL-24) during World War II, 18

Training
For aviation cadets in Texas in 1942, 2-3; operational training in Florida for newly commissioned aviators in 1943, 4-8; attrition rate in flight training, 9-10; preflight training to establish a pool of potential trainees during World War II, 11-12; between deployments in 1944-45, Carrier Air Group 31 trained at Hollister, California, 32-35; in 1946 former fighter pilots were retrained to fly battleship and cruiser floatplanes, 40; Hawkins's training enabled him to survive when he ejected from the cockpit of an F9F-6 Cougar in August 1953, 66-69, 71-72; in the mid-1950s OpNav made training films to provide naval personnel with a broader knowledge of their service, 74-75; in nuclear weapons delivery by A4D Skyhawk pilots in the late 1950s, 76-77, 79-80

Truk Atoll, Caroline Islands
Hit by U.S. carrier air strikes in February and April 1944, 19-21

VA-46
See Attack Squadron 46 (VA-46)

VF-31
See Fighter Squadron 31 (VF-31)

VF-191
See Fighter Squadron 191 (VF-191)

VX-5
See Experimental Squadron Five (VX-5)

Vietnam War
The Atsugi (Japan) Naval Air Station supported the war effort by doing a considerable amount of aircraft overhaul and repair work during the late 1960s, 98-99

Weather
Snow, fog, and cold created difficult flying conditions for U.S. pilots during the Korean War, 62-63

Winston, Lieutenant Commander Robert A., USN
Officer who commanded Fighter Squadron 31 and Air Group 31 during World War II and wrote a number of books on naval aviation, 14-15

Zero (Japanese Fighter Plane)
See A6M Zero

www.ingramcontent.com/pod-product-compliance
Lightning Source LLC
Chambersburg PA
CBHW080611170426
43209CB00007B/1395